What Is Consciousness?

NEW PARADIGM BOOKS OF
THE LASZLO INSTITUTE OF NEW PARADIGM RESEARCH
Kingsley L. Dennis, Series Editor

What Is Consciousness? Three Sages Look Behind the Veil
(June 2016)

What Is Reality? A New Map of Cosmos and Consciousness
(October 2016)

*The Laszlo Chronicle: A Global Thinker's Journey from
Systems to Consciousness and the Akashic Field*
(January 2017)

What Is Consciousness?

Three Sages Look Behind the Veil

Ervin Laszlo, Jean Houston, and Larry Dossey

FOREWORD BY STANLEY KRIPPNER

A NEW PARADIGM BOOK OF
THE LASZLO INSTITUTE OF NEW PARADIGM RESEARCH
Kingsley L. Dennis, Series Editor

SelectBooks, Inc.
New York

This edition published by SelectBooks, Inc.
For information address SelectBooks, Inc., New York, New York.

First Edition

ISBN 978-1-59079-347-3

Library of Congress Cataloging-in-Publication Data
Laszlo, Ervin, 1932-
What is consciousness? : three sages look behind the veil / Ervin Laszlo, Jean Houston, and Larry Dossey ; foreword by Stanley Krippner. -- First Edition.
    pages cm
Includes bibliographical references.
ISBN 978-1-59079-347-3 (hardbound book : alk. paper) 1. Consciousness. 2. Human beings. I. Houston, Jean. II. Dossey, Larry, 1940- III. Title.
B808.9.L37 2015
128'.2--dc23
                    2015033786

Book design by Janice Benight

Manufactured in the United States of America
10 9 8 7 6 5 4 3 2 1

Contents

✝
✝ ✝ ✝ ✝
✝ ✝ ✝ ✝
✝ ✝ ✝
✝

Foreword

There were six learned sages,
To study much inclined,
Who met to discuss Consciousness
(About it each was blind).
Each hoped by observation
To satisfy his mind.

The first sage thought of Consciousness,
Awake or in a dream,
As an experiential flow
With rivulets that seem
To be so fundamental that
"Consciousness is a stream."

The second sage knew of Consciousness
From his patients' anguish;
Their problems stemmed from urges
They tried hard to vanquish.
So, this great sage proclaimed that
"Consciousness is a wish."

The third followed Consciousness
Back to its primal lair.
He studied myths and legends
That led him to declare
"A Collective Consciousness
Is something we all share."

The fourth said the term Consciousness
Is faulty in the West.
In the East it is luminous,
And that word says it best;
Hence "Consciousness illuminates,
And also manifests."

For the fifth sage, Consciousness
Is entering a gate
By hypnosis, taking drugs,
Or pausing to meditate.
He concluded that "Consciousness
Is something like a state."

The sixth sage said "Consciousness
Is easy to explain.
Sight, smell, taste, and hunger,

Touch, sound and pain,
Are perceived, then Consciousness
Emerges from the brain."

Oft' in academic wars,
The disputants, it seems,
Rail on in sheer ignorance
Of what each other might mean,
And while some dissect Consciousness,
It still remains unseen.

THIS SPIN ON JOHN GODFREY SAXE'S NINETEENTH-CENTURY POEM "The Blind Men and the Elephant" describes the varying answers to the question: "What is consciousness?" The varying answers represent a significant development; however, that is often overlooked in contemporary discourse. After William James, arguably the founder of modern psychology in the United States, made consciousness a cornerstone of his investigations, the field was taken over by the behaviorists. For many decades, the prevailing dogma was that a phenomenon such as "consciousness" could only be discussed in subjective terms, and could not be properly studied by science with objective experimental methods.

This paradigm was dealt a death blow by the "cognitive revolution," which introduced methods of studying thought and other inner experiences that passed the scientific muster of its day. Cognitive psychology, and later, humanistic and transpersonal psychology, opened the door to the investigation of dreams, meditation, psychedelics, and other manifestations of consciousness. Soon, the cognitive, affective, and contemplative neurosciences solidified consciousness as a "respectable" topic for mainstream science. Psychoanalysis kept the flame of consciousness studies alive, as did European schools of psychology that never subscribed to behaviorist dogma.

There were positive aspects to the emphasis on limiting psychology to the study of externally observable behavior, however. Other animals could be considered in the psychological domain, as could infants and nonverbal adults, such as those incapacitated by physical or mental problems. In the meantime, the first recorded maps of consciousness could be found in the Indian *Upanishads,* dating back to the sixth century BCE, predating the Greek philosophers who laid the basis for Western inquiry on the topic (e.g., Plato's original distinction between sensory and abstract experiences).

The American Psychological Association *Dictionary of Psychology*'s definition of "consciousness" is twofold. The first describes consciousness as "the phenomena that humans report experiencing including mental contents ranging from sensory to somatic perception to mental images, reportable ideas, inner speech, intentions to act, recalled memories, semantics, dreams, hallucinations, emotional feelings, 'fringe' feelings (e.g., a sense of knowing), and aspects of cognitive and motor control." The second part of the definition speaks of "any of various subjective states of awareness in which conscious contents can be reported," giving examples of "altered states" such as sleeping, as well as the "global access function" of consciousness, presenting an endless variety of focal contents to executive control and decision making.[1]

This answer to the question "what is consciousness?" can serve as a useful introduction to the three brilliant chapters of this book. However, each of the authors uses the APA definitions, or aspects of them, as starting points for a much more comprehensive vision. Jean Houston places consciousness in the context of what she calls the "quantum nature of our universe," a revelation that has transformed human history. Houston has played a major role in this transformation, both with the small groups she has mentored and with international programs affiliated with the United Nations. For her, "consciousness is the quantum field of the cosmos, the basic reality of the world."

Larry Dossey has spent a lifetime contemplating and investigating consciousness. His chapter drives the nail in the coffin of the "physicalism doctrine," i.e., that "everything is physical, or as contemporary philosophers sometimes put it, that everything supervenes on, or is necessitated by, the physical."[2] In his carefully documented chapter, Dossey refutes this doctrine, presenting unanswered questions about the so-called "mind-body problem" that should bring a sense of modesty to anyone who claims that the problem can be answered by conventional data from the neurosciences. In his words, "empirical evidence shows that brains are separate, but minds are not." Developments in theoretical physics support Dossey's contentions, and he cites essays and articles by several Nobel Prize laureates.

Ervin Laszlo is equally articulate maintaining that consciousness is more than a product of our physiology. Conventional thinking limits the parameters of consciousness to sensory input, but Laszlo cites evidence from parapsychological research that indicates that there is communication "beyond the reach of the eye and ear." As my old friend Alan Watts was fond of saying, human beings are more than "skin-encapsulated egos." Laszlo goes even further, pointing out the holographic nature of consciousness, one that is consistent with some of the concepts of contemporary physics. His work is multidisciplinary, multicultural, and multinational, and comes from a perspective that is itself holographic.

I finished this book with a sense of awe and wonder. None of the authors resort to mystical musing or esoteric schema. Their models of reality are "evidence based," and many readers will be exposed to data they never knew existed. One of the joys of this book is discovery. Readers will have the opportunity to learn about themselves and the wondrous cosmic parade in which they valiantly carry their banners.

—STANLEY KRIPPNER
Alan Watts Professor of Psychology,
Saybrook University

What Is Consciousness?

Consciousness
Is the Quantum Field
of the Cosmos

———

BY JEAN HOUSTON

THE DISCOVERY OF THE QUANTUM NATURE of our universe changed the course of human history. Its profound revelations and implications cannot be overstated. Quantum theory demands a radical re-visioning of the role of consciousness as the underlying organizing principle of the universe. With this understanding, quantum physics is introducing us to ways of seeing that profoundly impact human thinking, feeling, sensing, knowing, and being. As Max Planck has commented, "I regard consciousness as fundamental. I regard matter as derivative from consciousness. We cannot get behind consciousness. Everything that we talk about, everything that we regard as existing, postulates consciousness."[1] The deeper knowledge of this, the kind taken not only into the mind, but into the heart, viscera, spirit and soul, changes us profoundly. It can radically affect us and bring us to our inherent possibilities for experiencing what I call our quantum identity and its foundation in quantum consciousness.

For many years, I have focused on developing human capacities in four areas: sensory/physical, psychological, mythical/narrative, and spiritual/unitive. I created thousands of exercises and practices to develop these capacities, resulting in many books and countless trainings and seminars, which I have been told, touch the lives of millions of people.

Now we face huge challenges and dangers that threaten our very existence. I have been moved to explore a way to meet enormous dangers with practices that enhance rather than destroy. We are in the time of evolve or perish. It would take something original and powerfully effective to activate our evolutionary genius. We have to go to the source of creativity itself, the great originating matrix that holds our potential genius and development.

For many years, I have been working with agencies of the United Nations and other international agents of personal and social change in 109 countries, helping develop social artists, leaders in many fields who seek an evolutionary model of personal and social change. I am promoting a new order in which universal awareness is applied to local concerns, and relationships—male and female, science and spirituality, economics and ecology, civic participation and personal growth and, ultimately, the self and the quantum field—come together in an interdependent matrix that benefits all.

We humans are not alone facing the massive transition that is upon us. Rather, we are embedded in a larger ecology of being, its motive force arising simultaneously from the planet that is our birthplace and the stars that are our destination. Pulsed by earth and universe toward a new stage of growth, we are waking up to the realization that we can become partners in creation—stewards of the earth's well-being and conscious participants in the cosmic epic of evolution. As ancient peoples have always known, the story is bigger than all of us, and yet requires our engagement, our love, and our commitment.

Over many years I have studied the cosmologies of ancient Hindu and Buddhist spirituality and indigenous shamanic practices of both. Despite their different metaphors, I found that they are both remarkably similar to findings of the frontiers of quantum physics. One discovers that in both ancient texts as well as shamanic practice, *consciousness* is central to the nature of reality.

In fact, a study of Eastern, Western, and many indigenous philosophies and world views provides keys and practices that deliver us not only from our chronic woes, but also bring us to our higher purpose as a member of an evolving universe. Then, too, the emerging understanding of reality introduced by quantum theory and the gathering evidence of the active role of consciousness in the world and cosmos not only bring about a basic paradigm shift, but give us the basis for a whole new story that is at once very ancient and ever new. This new paradigm offers a perspective on the natures of reality and consciousness that could influence much of the human agenda in science, mythology, theology, philosophy, psychology: the entire spectrum of our human condition. It may even provide the basis for a renaissance of self and society, a revolution in human possibilities beyond technological enhancements.

The universe has an outer body and an inner mind. The infrastructure of the mind mirrors the structures of the universe. When we are in certain states of consciousness, our minds can interact with the universe itself, in what the Buddhists call *interdependent co-arising.* These include meditation, contemplation, rapture, ecstasy, loving, trance, inspiration, and other altered states of mind. In these, one gains access to an unbounded awareness of the universal consciousness. The boundless self has many capacities beyond local consciousness. The deepest values, the deepest purpose, the deepest patterns for life are available. Within the level of creative patterns, not unlike the Platonic forms, one finds that great ideas and innovative actions become manifest. We have witnessed meditators, mystics and high creative persons who clearly see cosmic connections, the potential entry points into the cosmos, and return full of potential and creative ideas. Pioneers such as these are known to drop in an intent that sets up reverberations, which then come into the form of the things intended, because they are working with the quantum field that is perceived as a revelation from a higher source or cosmic consciousness. What is extraordinary is that when we can bring local consciousness to a higher resonance in the quantum field, we access news in and from the universe. In this state, all-knowing is direct knowing in real time, and all systems are go.

Mystics often experience a timeless, spaceless, polydimensional reality, in states of consciousness unfettered by ego needs or expectations. Thus the mystic, the high creative, or the meditator can choose from among the many perceived realities. The individual mind unites with the great, all-encompassing matrix consciousness that transcends all space-time categories.

In these states, we engage a beyond-space-time realm that is consonant with our deep mind or creative unconscious, from which everything arises. This is ultimately a spiritual experience and a quantum connection. It is all part of the great hologram, every part entangled with every other and working together. Quantum physics has discovered something that many mystics have long known, that our perception of the universe determines the very universe that is being observed. If we change the way we view the universe, the universe reflects this change back to us, because the universe is not separate from our perception of it. As Ervin Laszlo put it, "The world is not outside of me, and I am not outside of the world. The world is in me, and I am in the world."[2] Our creative imagination is truly divine, in that it affects the very blueprint of reality. It is the part of us through which God or the cosmic consciousness imagines this world into being. We appear to live in a universe of open-ended potential at each and every moment. We are partners in what is being dreamed up. How our universe manifests depends on how we both individually and collectively observe it. The real power, then, is in the viewing and our observation of the universe.

Similarly, it makes no sense to talk about the universe as if it exists separate from us, or to talk about us existing independently of the seemingly outer universe. As Larry Dossey observes, the "evidence overwhelmingly suggests that consciousness is both trans-spatial and trans-temporal, that it is *not in* space and time . . . brains are separate, but minds are not."[3] We are inseparable with the universe in a timeless embrace. We are dreaming up the universe while it is dreaming us up. This is what the Buddhists call interdependent co-arising.

But within this interdependence lies the human paradox. Here we are, local beings living in a space-time suit that allows us to persist for a number of years carrying out our earthly objectives. But we are also infinite beings with powers and possibilities that allow us to live in a universe larger than our aspirations and more fascinating than our dreams. In this time of great challenge, when the human experiment could come to an end within the next two centuries because of avarice and ignorance, the wonder is that principles and knowledge have arisen from science, cosmology, and the exploration of the nature of consciousness and spiritual reality. Beginning in the late nineteenth and early twentieth century, two phenomenal things happened almost simultaneously: the harvest of the wisdom of the world's spiritual traditions, and the revolution in physics that revealed to us the quantum nature of reality. My old friend Deepak Chopra wonderfully expressed what results from these two: "The future of God is the evolution of our own consciousness from separation to unity, from a fragmented mind to a whole mind, from thought which is in time to Awareness which is not in time."[4]

I have been working with these spiritual and scientific concepts to bring my hundreds of students to a higher level of consciousness and capacity. I might begin by showing them how they might connect with their quantum blueprint, the fullest expression of themselves. From this they realize that they are not, nor ever have been, alone. As Ervin Laszlo points out, "As a conscious human being, I am an intrinsic and infinite part of the consciousness that pervades the cosmos."[5]

I would then say, "So let us now explore the art of living in an expanded self that gives us access to latent or higher states of body functioning and mind states that enlighten, an enchanted state in which we consciously orchestrate our moods and emotions, our relationships, and all of our different and brilliant personalities and their corresponding skills.

"Be very present in your body as I speak to you now. Please know that your body is the stuff of stars and of the minerals of the earth. Your blood runs briny with the seas, the essence of oceans spills through your veins and arteries. The sediments of earth make up your cells. Your genes are universes in themselves, coded with enough information to recreate the world. It's these elements of earth and sky, nature and cosmos that actually compose your physical being—the inner mirror of the great nature that has pushed us to the choice points we now face. And it all has a purpose, even a destiny. You are, my friend, the apex of the 13.7-billion-year evolutionary process that has resulted in you and your life."

Then I would guide them into their quantum blueprint: "Your responsibility is to reconnect with this inner nature, this emergent evolutionary nature—this optimal template, this quantum blueprint, which has been waiting for you to recognize it and be filled by it. It is here, this quantum blueprint, looking for you, waiting for you.

"'Come closer, you say,' and it does. For each of you, its appearance will be unique. You may feel it as light, as joy, as something that is filled with the codes of your higher nature. It has been waiting for you to sense and recognize it as your higher destiny all these years, in your own local life and for millennia before that, since that first cosmic seed began to bloom. And now, the moment has come. Move toward it as the quantum blueprint moves toward you.

"Feel yourself connecting with its energy, its wondrous plans for you as you move into this blueprint of your quantum nature, your larger life. Connecting now with the energy and the plan for your larger life. As the optimal template moves in you, know that you are becoming a superb catalyst, a carrier of new genesis as the world is getting ready to move. Your mind is growing, so you can think in many ways—in words, in images, thoughts that border on genius, in fact can become genius. Much that you may have lost from your childhood and adolescence as well as those remarkable skills and qualities that were latent in you are now becoming real . . . courage, passion for the possible, rigor, diligence, a wave tide of joy and belief, the creative life, your spirit inspirited by the God, the cosmic consciousness, the Supreme Beloved who calls you into being. You are loved, nurtured, empowered, called forth to your highest destiny for this life in this time."

Given this initial entrance into the quantum blueprint, we can then have the sensibility and openness to explore life in the quantum universe. A good place to begin is with a new experience of time. As human beings, we are multitemporal by nature, and to explore the mystery of time within is to gain access to a universe larger than our aspiration, more complex than all our dreams. Let us take for example a quantum process I created, introducing the more fluid categories of space and time that operate in the psyche, which I call alternate temporal process (ATP). In this basic training process, one can experience subjective time in a compressed way. Adventures, writing books, finishing projects, voyaging in the seas of the unconscious, and learning or rehearsing things, activities that would normally take a long time, occur in a few minutes. This time process serves as the basis for the far more complex process that I will now introduce.

"Close your eyes and breathe deeply, inhale, exhale, inhale, exhale, following your breathing all the way in and all the way out . . . becoming more and more relaxed. Now I'm going to give you considerably more time than you need to do the following. You will have one minute of objective time, but with special time alteration, so that one minute experienced in subjective time will be as long as you need to live out a very interesting adventure. You may take a trip around the world, or visit a place you have long wanted to experience, or see old friends. Now these experiences may seem to take a minute, a day, a week, a month, or even years, but you will have all the time you need in subjective time, although only a minute of clock time will have passed. I will keep the time. Begin your experience now."

After one minute I call time and ask, "What did you experience?"

Most people report that their internal experiences seem a great deal longer than one minute, and for some, time itself becomes meaningless. The most common reported experience is a trip around the world. I have been astonished at the lavish, lengthy accounts of these one-minute world travelers. Once one is introduced to alternate time and time expansion, such feats, evidently natural to subjective time, becomes part of normal experience. Such alternate temporal experiences are possible because they are more in the order of experience that activates the right hemisphere of the brain, where clock time does not seem to operate. Rather, right-hemisphere time can be felt as timeless. The usual sense of time as passing belongs more to left-hemisphere brain processing.

For another quantum process, if you add several minutes more to alternate temporal process—say, three minutes of clock time equal to an hour or more of subjective time—you can imagine studying with a master to improve upon a skill that you y have, such as yoga, music, an athletic activity, writing, singing, teaching, dancing, etc. In teaching this, I have seen people making substantial improvements in so many areas of interest, even after they had been stuck for months or even years. The usual blocked state does not seem to operate in subjective time experiences.

As voyeur of the multiple realms of time, I have witnessed my students rehearse and improve skills that would normally take them months. Using ATP, my students have written novels, poems, and plays, completed doctoral dissertations, composed symphonies, improved their skills in yoga, golf, dancing, tennis, weaving, retrieved long-lost memories, and investigated in full detail possible futures and courses of action and selected ones to carry out. In more spiritual states of consciousness, time itself does not seem to exist. This brings us to the truly remarkable things you can do with "time travel" and changing the past and the probable future. But first, let us foray into some physics of quantum time.

Space-time and matter originate in the primordial quantum ground of infinite energy and quantum flux, and it constantly sustains them. There is no direction to time, neither past nor present nor future, but time past, time present, and time future occurring all together simultaneously, in ways that are difficult for us to understand, habituated as we are to present and future following relentlessly from the past with no side trips allowed. In the quantum world, all events can exist concurrently, and for all practical purposes, everything correlates with everything else. The universe is alive and interconnected through this quantum reality; as present scientific speculations suggests, information transmits through the bridges or wormholes connecting all points with all others in an indefinite number of possible patterns, constantly changing and turning on and off at incredible frequencies of up to 1,043 times per second. Either that, or we exist in a quantum hologram projected from beyond space-time, and within which we are all entangled and resonant with each other.

Ervin Laszlo, Brian Greene, and other physicists suggest that we are amphibious beings with regard to time and space, living several lives at the same time in a cosmic hologram. If you add to this the conundrum of certain aspects of quantum physics that suggest that all possible futures are here right now and that we stand at a crossroads in which we can select from one, while others go on in parallel universes—then you have a much more complex reality, unconscious to time. This would imply that in our so-called unconscious lies not only the repressed or forgotten experiences of our life, but also the experiences of ourselves in different dimensions of time and space.

Jennifer in one reality has Lyme disease. Jennifer in another does not, so she visits this alternate reality or time and consults with the healthy version of herself. She reports that she even had an experience of being in the healthy, disease-free body of her alternate self in the parallel world. When she returns, she is inspired or impacted with the experience; she immediately feels healthier, without the usual symptoms and fatigue, and then goes about finding the kind of medical help that helps her be rid of any remaining aspects of the disease.

We can easily dismiss this kind of phenomenon as the power of suggestion in an altered state of consciousness with psychosomatic effects. However, after having seen numerous examples of these kinds of learnings, changes, and shifts with several dozen students, you cannot close your accounts with reality and must conclude that something much more interesting is happening. If there is any truth to this matter, it is no wonder that we want to keep the lid on this multitemporal unconscious! Yet, perhaps these different worlds or times of our experience are not self-contained, but bleed through in other states of consciousness—dreams, reveries, creative inspirations, spiritual, and other potent experiences. The poets seem to know the same thing, but express it differently. T.S. Eliot writes in "Burnt Norton":

> Time present and time past
> Are both perhaps present in time future
> And time future contained in time past.[6]

And Walt Whitman writes in *Leaves of Grass* on crossing the eons of time and being with you, the reader:

> Full of life now, compact, visible,
> I, forty years old the eighty-third year of the States,
> To one a century hence or any number of centuries
>   hence,
> To you yet unborn these, seeking you.

> When you read these I that was visible am become
>   invisible,
> Now it is you, compact, visible, realizing my poems,
>   seeking me,
> Fancying how happy you were if I could be with you
>   and become your comrade;
> Be it as if I were with you. (Be not too certain but I
>   am now with you.)[7]

How do we bring ourselves into this expanded experience and use of time? Our understanding, based on quantum physics, of the simultaneity of times past, present, and future can be used in altered states of consciousness to "change" a minor happening in a person's past so that it affects their present and future in positive new ways. In a sense, one is editing the Akashic field and record.

We can remember and even re-create the past and the future. Memories can be changed on this simultaneous continuum in which the universe, including all times, experiences, and dimensions, can be changed, transformed, rewritten, re-experienced, because the universe is regenerating itself every nanosecond. Since we are conscious participants in the living universe, we can enter the Akashic fields of memory and shift elements of our own history. Here are several examples of how this is done.

My associate Peggy Rubin was born in the midst of the Great Depression to struggling farmers in south Texas. Once highly esteemed Methodist ministers in Korea in the 1930s, they were forced to leave the country for advocating an end to the Japanese colonization, and wound up on a family farm in south Texas. They showed little talent for farming, thus their poverty. Later, Peggy learned from her mother that her father did not welcome the news of her pending arrival, and greeted her birth as just another burden. Her parents were kind enough to her during her childhood, but Peggy was always aware of an underlying sadness, even distance, in her childhood. This affected her life in small and large ways especially when it came to her own self-worth. She said to me, "If only I could experience their having some moments of joy when my mother told my dad that I was 'in the oven.'"

So, using the technique of tuning into the quantum dimension of time, Peggy experienced their moments of joy at her coming. So vivid was her "new" recollection that she felt the release of her burdened self-image and has been able to open to encouraging new arenas in her life and relationships. In fact, to my mind and many others, she has become one of the great teachers of our time.

Recently, she visited her elder brother and sister and found that they too were much warmer and welcoming to her then they had ever been. Something had shifted that affected the whole nature of her relationships and self-image. Through this quantum process she had edited the Akashic field, the great record of the universe in which the events of her life had been entered.

Changing what one perceives as relatively minor things in one's past (not deaths or radically tragic or traumatic happenings) seems to affect one's present life and circumstance in remarkable ways that demonstrate the fluidity of time in one's life. The process of shifting the nature of events in one's life can be applied in many ways, even for rapidly learning new skills. Here, for example, is my story of working with this process.

As a child, thinking myself musical, I took up the piano. Unfortunately, with my father's work as a comedy writer for the big comedians of the day, we were always on the road, rarely in the same place for more than a few weeks, or months at most. Wherever we traveled, when it came to my piano lessons, I found myself stuck in the same miserable piece—"The Little Glow Worm." In Los Angeles, my piano teacher, Miss Sturges, asked, "And what piece are you working on now Jean, dear?"

Me, sullenly: "'The Little Glow Worm.'"

Miss Fortin, in New York: "And what piece are you studying?"

Me, resentfully: "The stinking 'Little Glow Worm.'"

And so it went from town to town, stuck in the purgatory of the same piece. So, after seeing the success of so many of my students using this time and memory replacement strategy, I decided to try it myself. What if I had taken up the violin instead? That instrument could be carried around and I could practice on the trains on which we constantly traveled, and I did not have to rely on the occasional piano. So I put myself in the quantum field of memory, where I had become proficient on the violin. After a while, I barely remembered my attempts at the piano. I then took actual violin lessons with my teacher, who was very surprised at how quickly I was learning. "Surely, Jean," she said, "you must have had lessons. You are too far along in violin not to have had them!" And of course I had had the lessons and the practice, but in the world of the quantum change in memory. After two months of weekly lessons with my violin teacher I was playing *Pachelbel's Canon*.

Here is how I guide this process.

"Let us now choose something in our lives that we would like to edit and re-create. Please, not a major incident, but one, perhaps like the ones I just described, where little changes could have surprising results both in your memory as well as long term outcomes in your mood and perception and capacities. For this, it would be best that you stand, but if that is not convenient then do this process in your chair.

"I want you to place your hands in front of you as if you were pushing against something. It is not a hard surface but feels more like vibrations, the frequencies of a different time in your life. All of the times in your life are present. So you may see or feel there yourself as a baby, your life in your teens, and so on. But now, moving through these frequencies of time, begin to feel yourself in the realm of memory. Recall now an incident in your past that you would like to edit. Not a major incident, please, but one that, if shifted somewhat, could have been more positive and helpful than the one you remember. So for example, instead of the teacher telling you that you had no talent for art, she would say, 'What an interesting drawing, a house that looks like a fat person. What a great idea! Please add more to the drawing. I am fascinated by what you are doing!' Or, if your Mom or Dad were about to give you a spanking, you might change the story by saying, 'I know I did something that hurt my brother, but let's bring him in so I can tell him how really sorry I am that I hurt him, and then we can all be friends.'

"You get the idea. You shift the story to a positive, even creative, event. And you keep on playing, even enacting, that new scenario over and over again, until it holds and become a realistic part of your memory, stronger and more vibrant than the old memory."

While conducting this time-shifting practice, I have had cases of students whose new memories were so strong that they crossed over to other people who were involved, and even some of them began to remember the shifted memory as the actual one. That is how you edit the quantum field, the Akashic record.

So, back to the process:

"With your hands out, feel yourself pushing through the curtain of time. It is an energetic field, carrying the vibration and frequencies of your history. Go now to the old memory, observing it without any particular emotion, like watching a movie while eating popcorn. You watch and see what needs to be changed and how you will change it to your benefit and advantage. As you re-image the new story, also act it out. Really act it out, using your body and gestures and emotions to play out the new version. Once you have done that, do it again, and then again until it 'takes' and you feel the reality in the vibrational field of new memory. When this session ends do this process again, several times in the next week or longer until the new memory is the one that you remember, and the old memory is like a faded dream, if it is still in your mind at all."

One can use a similar process to select a particular intention to manifest in the future. This comes under the rubric of the art and science of manifestation and has to do with how we turn possibilities into probabilities.

Why do things happen? I am not speaking here of the out-of-the-way surprises that occasionally and randomly rain on us. I am referring to the ways in which certain probabilities seem to follow us throughout our lives. In physics they are called probability waves or curves. For any event there are many possibilities. The emphasis given to a possibility wave increases the likelihood of it becoming a probability wave, and that probability which you intend starts happening in space and time. If you learn to orchestrate your consciousness in a certain way, practice a kind of yoga of the mind, or working with the quantum field, then you will find that you can change possibilities, alter outcomes, and even enable outcomes to flow, as new and thickened possibility waves that lead to intended probabilities. By holding onto the possibility, you are propagating a wave that moves and vibrates and undulates through space, and it would also seem, through time—that is, time in which past, present, and future exist simultaneously.

According to some of the most recent work in the new physics, this wave of possibility enters time past, present, and future. Time is not a one-way river, according to quantum principles. This fact shocks our mind for we are so conditioned to believe in time's arrow.

The exercise is to imagine the reality that you intend, that is, the thing or occasion that you wish to manifest. That is a possibility wave but not yet a probability one. So you have to thicken the probability. I might say to a participant,

> "Please imagine your intention so dramatically that it overrides all your old feelings of doubt and dilemma. Observe how your active imagination offers you enjoyable images, feelings, and story lines that exceed old ways of thinking and doing. Now let's bring in more of the probability factor. You do this by inviting the quantum field of all potentials to join you in the creation of your intention. Invite it in. Call it in. Reach out, even, and bring its tides and powers into your own local field. Swim in it. Enjoy the paradox of being local but also nonlocal, human, and god-stuff incarnate in space and time.

> "You are the local imagination immersed in the great field of imaginal creation. By your invitation, the universe, with its infinite ideas and treasures, is able to help you now, to fill in the gaps, as well as expand your intention. The quantum field in its dramatizing power arises in you with special effects and soul-crafting images and ideas. Receive them and play them out! Play them out and enact them until you get the feeling tone that it is happening. Feeling tone is a special

kind of click in your consciousness that says, "Ok, it is so. It is happening." Put your hands out and have the sense of calling in, winding it, being entangled with and thus receiving the appropriate people, opportunities, resources that are coming together now to make your intention a reality in your space-time zone, as it has already been confirmed in the zone of the quantum holofield. There is really no distinction between the two and when you know that, your intended reality can move right in.

"Do all this and put it to music and dance if you are so inclined. I have found out that rhythm and movement have a wondrous salutary effect on the arts of manifestation. So, if you wish, imagine it vividly, feel it, sense its happening, play it out and then, dramatize and dance it, sing it, know it to be and to be happening. Movement is really important as movement produces endorphins—those joyous, positive, top-of-the-world hormones that raise your happiness quotient and let the universe partner you in promising and extraordinary ways. (As an example of this, go to a Gospel church and watch the momentum of possibility happening through the movement, the rhythm, the singing.) The point is you have caused your body and mind, your very consciousness, to slip out of its same-old-same-old thoughts and expectations. You have moved from the imagination to the imaginal, which is part of the universal consciousness field of all potentials."

What I am doing is helping the participant to activate creativity and manifestation. In this, imagination is central. But even our imagination is transcended by the universe, and when it operates in us, we are no longer simply imaginative. We are imaginal. We are in the quantum holofield of consciousness. We are no longer caught in our own habits and expectations. We are given the blueprints, the guidance, forms, and patterns of what up to now we have only imagined, however vividly. Up to now, we have mostly operated out of imagination, and now we are ready to operate out of imaginal quantum creativity. Immanuel Kant talked about productive and reproductive imagination. Reproductive is imagination, as we understand it, drawn from our experiences in life. Productive imagination means a direct line to the universal consciousness with its imaginal guiding forces.

When you see a Mozart, a Shakespeare, a Goethe, or a da Vinci, an Einstein, a Georgia O'Keefe, a Madame Curie, or a Margaret Mead, or all the extraordinary people who have tapped into something that breaks the bonds of the usual human condition, what are they doing? All my life I have read Shakespeare. How in the world did he come up with all this passionate, profound and worldmaking language that few other language masters ever possessed? The same is true of Goethe in the German language. What was going on with them? I believe that along with their astonishing genius, they entered into the imaginal sources of language and drama. How do you get from imagination to imaginal? We have been doing this by our training in working with quantum powers which help source the imaginal world. It is also very important to build internal structures that can support the imaginal.

There are four levels to take you to quantum support: physical-sensory, psychological, mythic-symbolic, and spiritual-unitive.

I tell my students, "In the first or physical and sensory realm you build up inner sensory systems. Start, for example, with inner taste. You chew on apples in your mind. You feel the juice bursting between your teeth. Pop a sunflower seed in your mouth and crunch it down. Have a salad of wild greens that bites you back, chastened by a little bit of olive oil and a touch of lemon. Now taste the idea or intention that you wish to manifest.

"Now for inner touch. Feel the long bony nose of a horse. Plunge both hands into a barrel of potato chips and break up as many as you can. Walk through a vat of warm honey. Now feel the intention as it comes into actuality.

"Now inner smell. Smell a rose garden. Smell an Italian restaurant. Add your own smell sensations and then smell the intention and its aroma of success.

"Now inner sight. See a sunrise. See an apple tree in full bloom. Go further. See a bevy of medieval nuns in great wimples walking two-by-two through a medieval herb garden. See a child smile. See now your intention in its fullness.

"Inner hearing. Hear the wind rushing through the trees. Hear the pounding of the waves on a beach. Hear the tapping of high heels on the floor. Hear the rooster crow in the morning.

"Now hear, touch, taste, smell and see what it is you intend, what you wish to accomplish.

"The second level, the psychological level, has to do with a shift in your identity, not the usual ego-bound notion of the self, but rather bringing in one of the many selves that accompany you, selves that do not have your particular ego's history of doubt and distress. There is simply a purer, more open, and available self within you. For example, I do not like to write. In fact, I am almost phobic about writing. But I love to cook and am quite a good cook. I have virtually no blocks around cooking. Not so for writing. And yet I am closing in on almost thirty published books and a great deal of unpublished material.

"How do I do this? I immerse myself entirely within the persona of a cook. Then, at the computer, I think entirely in cooking images, stirring the sauce that embodies the book, adding the spices of new and varied associations. I bring the cook's creativity and energy to myself as a writer."

Here are some of the practices that I suggest to my students. They can make a list of other personae with particular skills that they possess. If I made such a list it would include a teacher, cook, traveler, UN and cultural advisor, good friend, dog lover, reader, healer, comedian, people-gatherer, dramatist, risk-taker, occasional shaman, midwife of souls, wild woman, social art-ist. I ask you to do the same. Write a list of some of your own personae. Then from this list choose one or more, not more than three. Get inside each persona, one at a time. Feel the way they look at the world, given their particular skills. Experience yourself embodied within each character, possessing his or her way of looking and acting in the world. It often helps to do this to music. Make the motions of your persona in action. So if it is a sculptor, begin sculpting, if a dancer, start dancing.

Then bring this persona with its skills and ways of being in the world to your particular desire or intention. Just as I become a cook so I can write, so can you bring this other per-sona to experience and act out the intention that you desire. When I become a cook, the words I need to write begin to flow, they simmer in my mind like a fine soup, they emerge as a grand coconut cake, they provide a sumptuous feast. The feast, however, is one of ideas and images and solutions, and above all, words—words that move like wands, words that work! I want you to do the same.

Then there is the mythic level, where you become hero or heroine in the great adventure of making your intention man-ifest. Consider yourself on a road of adventure and discovery. You are larger than your ordinary life; accept it. And accept the helpers—both natural and supernatural—who are there to assist you. They may show up in many interesting forms—ani-mals, angels, numinous borderline persons, and above all, your entelechy, your higher guidance, who is providing direction as well as opening up pathways to new possibilities. You get beyond the dark woods of unbelief and enter shining castles where you are recognized as a great one, gifted with tools and treasures to accomplish your aim. You may discover archetypal friends and supporters who can be gods or goddesses, legendary figures, powers of virtue and intelligence—the archetype of all-giving love, the archetype of intelligence and discernment, the archetype of abundance, the archetype of healing.

Archetypes are many things—primal forms, codings of the deep unconscious, constellations of psychic energy, patterns of relationship. Above all, they are the symbolic projections of higher consciousness. As major organs of the psyche, archetypes give us our essential connections; without them we would lose the gossamer bridge that joins spirit with nature, mind with body, and self with the metabody of the universe. Archetypes are organs of essence, the cosmic blueprints of How It All Works. Because they contain so much, archetypes bewilder analysis and perhaps can only be known by direct experience.

As we participate in the journey of transformation and the acquisition of quantum powers, we actively engage in archetypal existence. We form a powerful sense of identity with the archetypal character, and this mythic being becomes an aspect of ourselves writ large. Symbolic happenings appear with undisguised relevance, not only for our own lives and problems, but for the remaking of society, as well. Working with myth and archetype, we discover that we are characters in the drama of cosmic consciousness, the *anima mundi*, the 'soul of the world.' In this discovery we push the boundaries of our own human story and gain the courage to live mythically and help heal our world.

Archetypes, then, are the very principles that hold the world's wisdom and understanding. They are best introduced and mediated by your entelechy, your higher guidance. As you enter into resonance with your entelechy, you feel its love and affirmation of you. Once that is truly and strongly apparent, step into the entelechy; feel yourself suffused with its powers; then, make a quarter-turn and ask it to introduce you to an archetype who can support and help you. This archetype may have a name and an identity from one of the great archetypes of other cultures—Athena, the archetype of wisdom; Apollo, archetype of light and enlightenment; Merlin, the high magus and wizard who makes things happen; or Quan Yin, the archetype of compassion. Or it may have no special name, but embody particular powers and capacities. It may be closer to the quantum realm and its powers than we are in our normal human lives. In the ancient Tibetan Buddhist scriptures archetypes are known sometimes as *yidams*—rivers to the source of all reality. By engaging the support of the archetypal friend, we find a greater ease and flow in our journey of discovery and manifestation. We discover, too, that our intention, especially if it is one of service to enhancement and the world, is easier to manifest more quickly.

Finally, there is the spiritual level, the place of the One Consciousness, the source of it all, the Akashic superimplicate order, the beyond-space-time source of space-time quantum reality. In reaching this level you feel a drenching that cleanses your entire being. The regrets and sorrows of your life seem to be washed away, and your mind is as clear and luminous as the dawn sky. You move into the realm that seems to contain everything. You have only to think of something and it appears. You have entered the Mind of the Maker—the Creative Force at the center of all there is.

Realities sweep through—stars and starfish, icebergs and ice cream, mountains and microchips, dolphins and daisies, geysers and galaxies. Creation in its unending abundance, and even the manifestation of your own dream. The universe is holding its breath, waiting to take you to a higher and more evolved place in the cosmic order of things.

Consciousness is the quantum field of the cosmos: the basic reality of the world. *Your* consciousness is a precious shoot, a green tendril of this enormous Oneness beyond-space-time.

Consciousness Is Eternal, Infinite, and One— A Summing Up

by Larry Dossey

One night when I was six, I lay sleepless in our farmhouse on the bleak central Texas prairie. I peered out the window at the canopy of stars shimmering in the night sky. I vividly remember the astonishment of being *aware* of them. Although I did not know grown-up words such as "consciousness," I was simply amazed that I could *know* something, anything. My mind could have been a complete blank, but it wasn't; yet, *why* did there appear to be something rather than nothing? What was this awareness thing, and where did it come from? If no one were aware of anything, would anything still be there? And where did my awareness go when I went to sleep? These thoughts returned night after night, but never with any answers.

Perhaps you too experienced thoughts like these as a child, because they involve archetypal questions that have surfaced throughout recorded history. They can be distilled to the basic query that is the title of this book: *What is consciousness?*

Different cultures have found various ways of exploring this great question. An approach I favor is not to define meticulously what consciousness is (as if this were possible), but to describe how consciousness behaves, how it shows itself, how it manifests in the world. Scientists do this routinely. For example, physicists can't really say what an electron is, but they have discovered features such as its mass, velocity, charge, and how it behaves under certain conditions. We can approach consciousness in the same way. We may not be able to offer a precise definition, but we can observe how it manifests in people's lives and in actual experiments, then form opinions about its nature, origin and destiny.

Despite our best efforts, however, our knowledge of consciousness will always be incomplete and therefore tinged with mystery. I am happy to acknowledge mystery in life, and I hope you are too, because this will assist us as we proceed by making us more flexible and less dogmatic. Mystery is ineradicable, and creatures with limited, finite intelligence—all of us—will do well to make peace with mystery early on. I choose to celebrate mystery, because in doing so it becomes friendlier and less formidable. Mystery, after all, is the source of surprise and delight on those extraordinary occasions when the unknown becomes known. On heavy wooden beams of a hallway in our home, I have stenciled in Old English script a statement that honors mystery: "Something unknown is doing we don't know what." This observation always makes me smile and is my way of bowing to the great unknowns. It is a comment by astrophysicist Sir Arthur Eddington referring to certain baffling features of quantum physics, but I like to apply it to life in general.

Our human limitations also warrant humility. William James, the father of American psychology and one of the great modern investigators of consciousness, understood the need for humility in this task. He was concerned with not only what we know, but what we *can* know. James must have been a pet lover. He said:

> I firmly disbelieve, myself, that our human experience is the highest form of experience extant in the universe. I believe rather that we stand in much the same relation to the whole of the universe as our canine and feline pets do to the whole of human life. They inhabit our drawing-rooms and libraries. They take part in scenes of whose significance they have no inkling. They are merely tangent to curves of history the beginnings and ends and forms of which pass wholly beyond their ken. So we are tangents to the wider life of things.[1]

James was not alone in his view of human limitations. Albert Einstein, James's contemporary, observed, "My religiosity consists in a humble admiration of the infinitely superior spirit that reveals itself in the little that we, with our weak and transitory understanding, can comprehend of reality."[2] And, "Two things are infinite, the universe and human stupidity, and I am not yet completely sure about the universe."[3]

For those readers who nonetheless want to carry with them an image or definition of consciousness through the pages that follow, I offer the following observation from one of India's preeminent contemporary philosophers and consciousness researchers, K. Ramakrishna Rao. Many Western scientists and philosophers share Professor Rao's views, as we shall see:

> Consciousness in the Indian tradition is more than an experience of awareness. It is a fundamental principle that underlies all knowing and being. . . . The cognitive structure does not generate consciousness; it simply reflects it; and in the process limits and embellishes it. In a fundamental sense, consciousness is the source of our awareness. In other words, consciousness is not merely awareness as manifest in different forms but it is also what makes awareness possible. It is said in *Kena Upaniṣad* that consciousness is the ear of the ear, the thought of the thought, the speech of the speech, the breath of the breath and the eye of the eye. . . . Consciousness is the light which illumines the things on which it shines.[4]

I never outgrew my childhood fascination with consciousness. My interest became more intense. This infatuation has followed me throughout my career as an internal medicine physician steeped in the life sciences. Much of my adult life has been spent taking care of sick, dying, and wounded patients in emergency rooms, critical care units, and battlefields. These experiences have brought questions about consciousness into sharpened focus, and they have intensified the relevance of consciousness in my own life. In this journey, a picture of consciousness has evolved for me: consciousness as eternal, infinite, and one.

For your consideration, here are some of the reasons why.

Despite the towering intellectual and technological achievements of twentieth-century science, its spell over us has been irreversibly weakened. There are at least two important reasons for this. First, scientist and layman alike have become aware of the limits and shortcomings of scientific knowledge. Second, we realize that our perpetual hunger for spiritual understanding is real and undeniable. It can neither be defined away by subtle logic, nor be satisfied by viewing the universe as sterile, mechanistic, and accidental.[5]

—ROGER S. JONES, *Physics as Metaphor*

The most urgent issue we humans face is how we conceive ourselves—whether as complex lumps of matter guided by the so-called blind, meaningless laws of nature, or as creatures who, although physical, are also imbued with something more: consciousness, mind, will, choice, purpose, direction, meaning and spirituality, that difficult-to-define quality that says we are connected with something that transcends our individual self and ego. Every decision we make is influenced by how we answer this great question: Who are we?

There is growing awareness that the endless arguments between proponents of these two views are more than hair-splitting disagreements among experts, but they have real consequences for our future on earth, and perhaps whether we shall have a future.[6] As novelist and statesman André Malraux (1901–1976) said, the twenty-first century will be spiritual, or it will not be.[7]

Václav Havel (1936–2011), the author, poet, playwright and diplomat who was the first president of the Czech Republic, saw a hell looming in our world and had the guts to say so on the international stage. As a potential solution, he said, "It seems to me that one of the most basic human experiences, one that is genuinely universal and unites—or, more precisely, could unite—all of humanity, is the experience of transcendence in the broadest sense of the word."[8] Havel endorsed what he called "responsibility to something higher." In a speech to a joint session of the United States Congress on February 21, 1990, he said:

> Consciousness precedes Being, and not the other way around. . . . [F]or this reason, the salvation in this human world lies nowhere else than in the human heart. . . . Without a global revolution in the sphere of human consciousness, nothing will change for the better in the sphere of our being

as humans, and the catastrophe toward which this world is headed—be it ecological, social, demographic or a general breakdown of civilization—will be unavoidable. If we are no longer threatened by world war or by the danger that the absurd mountains of accumulated nuclear weapons might blow up the world, this does not mean that we have definitely won. We are still capable of understanding that the only genuine backbone of all our actions, if they are to be moral, is responsibility. *Responsibility to something higher* than my family, my country, my company, my success—responsibility to the order of being where all our actions are indelibly recorded and where and only where they will be properly judged [emphasis added].[9]

There are vibrant developments in key areas of science that show real promise in humankind's search for, and responsibility to, something higher. There are solid reasons to believe that Havel's "global revolution in the sphere of human consciousness" may be closer than we think—that, after three centuries of a flirtation with and seduction by a purely physical view of who we are, another view is emerging.

THE FACE OF PHYSICALISM

Physicalism is the doctrine that the real world consists simply of the physical world. Its sibling is materialism, the doctrine that nothing exists except matter and its movements and modifications, and that consciousness and will are wholly due to material agency.[10] These terms—physicalism and materialism—are often used interchangeably, as I shall do here (with apologies to my philosopher friends who may cringe at this generalization).

What do physicalism and materialism actually look like? They involve a multifaceted view in which, as astrophysicist David Lindley has said, "We humans are just crumbs of organic matter clinging to the surface of one tiny rock. Cosmically, we are no more significant than mold on a shower curtain."[11] In this view, spirituality, the sense of connectedness with something that transcends the individual self, is equated with self-deception, fantasy, hallucination, or sheer stupidity; meaning, direction, and free will are absent. As philosopher Daniel Dennett puts it, "When we consider whether free will is an illusion or reality, we are looking into an abyss. What seems to confront us is a plunge into nihilism and despair."[12] In this worldview, there is no purpose to anything. As molecular biologist and Nobel laureate Jacques Monod (1910–1976) stated, "The cornerstone of scientific method is . . . the systematic denial that 'true' knowledge can be got at by interpreting phenomena in terms of final causes—that is to say, of 'purpose.'"[13]

Physicalism involves the presumption that the everyday idea of mind is an exaggerated, unnecessary concept. As philosopher Dennett says without a whiff of irony in his book *Consciousness Explained*, "We're all zombies. Nobody is conscious."[14] Nobel Prize–winning molecular biologist Francis

Crick confidently proclaimed, "[A] person's mental activities are entirely due to the behavior of nerve cells, glial cells, and the atoms, ions, and molecules that make up and influence them."[15] Similarly, astronomer Carl Sagan unequivocally stated, "[The brain's] workings—what we sometimes call mind—are a consequence of its anatomy and physiology, and nothing more."[16] And as psychiatrist and sleep researcher Allan Hobson asserted, "Consciousness, like sleep, is of the Brain, by the Brain, and for the Brain."[17] In sum, physicalism and materialism constitute a bleak vision in which, as Nobel Prize-winning physicist Steven Weinberg said, "The more the universe seems comprehensible, the more it also seems pointless."[18]

One of the bleakest descriptions of the physicalist panorama is that of philosopher-mathematician Lord Bertrand Russell:

> That man is the product of causes which had no prevision of the end they were achieving; that his origin, his growth, his hopes and fears, his loves and his beliefs, are but the outcome of accidental collocations of atoms; that no fire, no heroism, no intensity of thought or feeling, can preserve an individual life beyond the grave; that all the labours of the ages, all the devotion, all the inspiration, all the noonday brightness of human genius, are destined to extinction in the vast death of the solar system; and the whole temple of Man's achievement must inevitably be buried beneath the debris

of a universe in ruins—all these things, if not quite beyond dispute, are yet so nearly certain, that no philosophy that rejects them can hope to stand. Only within the scaffolding of these truths, only on the firm foundation of unyielding despair, can the soul's habitation henceforth be safely built.[19]

A few science insiders have considered religion and spirituality as relatively immune from the corrosive influence of physicalism. For example, in his 1929 Swarthmore Lecture, astrophysicist Sir Arthur Eddington remarked, "Dismiss the idea that natural law may swallow up religion; it cannot even tackle the multiplication table single-handed."[20]

Others suggest that the intractable mind-versus-matter debate rests on semantic misunderstandings and is overblown. Among them is the British anti-materialist philosopher Mary Midgley, who said:

> The real trouble with the mind-body problem centers on the word "materialism." This word is itself a relic of dualism: it suggests that there are two rival stuffs—mind and matter—competing to be seen as basic to the world. It tells us to choose one of these and reduce the other to it. There are not two such separate stuffs. There is just a complex world containing complex creatures, about whom many sorts of questions arise. Each question must

be answered in its own terms. . . . But actually
our thoughts are quite as real as our coffee cups,
and "matter" is every bit as obscure a concept as
"mind."[21]

It has been difficult to find traction in this debate. The
dominant physicalist view— that mind and consciousness are
products of brain function—is served up within contemporary
science not as a modest hypothesis or humble conjecture, but
as an incontrovertible fact, and anyone who disagrees is likely
to be considered an apostate or traitor to science. As consciousness researcher Edward F. Kelly, of the University of Virginia,
states in the landmark book *Beyond Physicalism*,

[These] well-meaning defenders of Enlighten-
ment-style rationalism . . . clearly regard themselves, and current mainstream science itself, as
reliably marshaling the intellectual virtues of reason and objectivity against retreating forces of
irrational authority and superstition. For them the
truth of the [physicalist view] has been demonstrated beyond reasonable doubt, and to think
anything different is necessarily to abandon centuries of scientific progress, release the black flood
of occultism, and revert to primitive supernatu-
ralist beliefs characteristic of bygone times.[22]

Mathematician and philosopher Charles Eisenstein has drawn attention to the condescending mindset that typifies materialists who hold this view:

> The unfalsifiable world-view of the [materialist] Skeptic extends far beyond scientific paradigms to encompass a very cynical view of human nature. The debunker must buy into a world full of frauds, dupes, and the mentally unstable, where most people are less intelligent and less sane than he is, and in which apparently honest people indulge in the most outrageous mendacity for no good reason. For the witnesses are, on the face of it, sincere. How can I account for their apparent sincerity? I have to assume either (1) that this apparent sincerity is a cynical cover for the most base or fatuous motives, or (2) they are ignorant, incapable of distinguishing truth from lies and delusion.[23]

The cynicism that Eisenstein identifies is liberally seasoned with arrogance. Sir John C. Eccles (1903–1997), the Nobel Prize–winning neurophysiologist, was one of the twentieth century's most vigorous opponents of physicalism in the debate over the nature of consciousness. He found arrogance to be endemic in this discourse, and he considered it a pathological pollutant—literally a disease:

Arrogance is one of the worst diseases of scientists and it gives rise to statements of authority and finality which are expressed usually in fields that are completely beyond the scientific competence of the dogmatist. It is important to realize that dogmatism has now become a disease of scientists rather than of theologians.[24]

"Beats the Heck Out of Me"

I must say, modern discussions about the mind are astoundingly parochial. Physicists advocate QM [quantum mechanics], biologists neurons, and good computationalists like myself, computers, each looking with bemused condescension upon their eccentric neighbors. Can we not get some bakers to participate in this forum, who will advocate that the roots of consciousness reside in the eclair?[25]

—Joshua Stern, *computer scientist*

The dogma of materialism suffers from two fatal defects: the sheer poverty of evidence that brains produce consciousness; and the enormous human costs of a world that is sanitized of a spiritual outlook, which the dogma forbids.

No human has ever seen a brain or anything else produce consciousness, and there is no accepted theory as to how this *could* happen. The link between a brain and consciousness is as mysterious today as it was when Thomas Henry Huxley wrote in 1886: "How it is that anything so remarkable as a state of consciousness comes about as a result of irritating nervous tissue, is just as unaccountable as the appearance of the djinn when Aladdin rubbed his lamp in the story."[26] The weakness of the brain-makes-consciousness dogma has become obvious to an increasing number of top-tier scientists, as the following comments demonstrate. I include several examples to show that these are not isolated opinions.

Steven Pinker, experimental psychologist at Harvard University, on how consciousness might arise from something physical, such as the brain, stated, "Beats the heck out of me. I have some prejudices, but no idea of how to begin to look for a defensible answer. And neither does anyone else."[27] Neurophysiologist Roger Sperry concurs: "Those centermost processes of the brain with which consciousness is presumably associated are simply not understood. They are so far beyond our comprehension at present that no one I know of has been able even to imagine their nature."[28] Eugene P. Wigner also observes, "We have at present not even the vaguest idea how to connect the physio-chemical processes with the state of mind,"[29] while fellow physicist Freeman J. Dyson adds, "the origin of life is a total mystery, and so is the existence of human consciousness. We have no clear idea how the electrical discharges occurring in nerve cells in our brains are connected with our feelings and desires and actions."[30] Mathematical physicist Sir Roger Penrose declares: "My position [on consciousness] demands a major revolution in physics. . . . I've come to believe that there is something very fundamental missing from current science. . . . Our understanding at this time is not adequate and we're going to have to move to new regions of science. . . ."[31]

One of the patriarchs of quantum physics, Nobel laureate Niels Bohr, conceded: "We can admittedly find nothing in physics or chemistry that has even a remote bearing on consciousness. . . . [Q]uite apart from the laws of physics and chemistry, as laid down in quantum theory, we must also consider laws of quite a different kind."[32] His contemporary, Nobel laureate and physicist Werner Heisenberg, similarly observed: "There can be no doubt that 'consciousness' does not occur in physics and chemistry, and I cannot see how it could possibly result from quantum mechanics."[33]

Even pioneering neurosurgeon Wilder Penfield insists that "it will always be quite impossible to explain the mind on the basis of neuronal action within the brain. . . . Although the content of consciousness depends in large measure on neuronal activity, awareness itself does not. . . . To me, it seems more and more reasonable to suggest that the mind may be a distinct and different essence."[34] Finally, Sir John Maddox, editor of the prestigious journal *Nature* for twenty-two years, points out: "What consciousness consists of . . . is . . . a puzzle. Despite the marvelous successes of neuroscience in the past century. . . we seem as far from understanding cognitive process as we were a century ago."[35]

THE GHASTLY SILENCE

One of the most forceful descriptions of the failure of modern science to come to terms with conscious experience comes from Nobel Prize–winning physicist Erwin Schrödinger:

> The scientific picture of the real world around me is very deficient. It gives a lot of factual information, puts all our experience in a magnificently consistent order, but it is ghastly silent about all and sundry that is really near to our heart that really matters to us. It cannot tell us a word about red and blue, bitter and sweet, physical pain and physical delight; it knows nothing of beautiful and ugly, good or bad, God and eternity. Science sometimes pretends to answer questions in these domains, but the answers are very often so silly that we are not inclined to take them seriously.[36]

Dedicated physicalists do not agree with these dismissive comments. Some physicalists tout hypotheses or theories which they claim show decisively that the brain makes consciousness. So it is not quite right to say that physicalism has no theories about the origins of consciousness; we should say, rather, that physicalism has no *successful* theories for such. Astrophysicist David Darling describes this impasse:

> [A] growing number of scientists are now busily rummaging around in the brain trying to explain

how the trick of consciousness is done. Researchers of the stature of Francis Crick, Daniel Dennett, Gerald Edelman, and Roger Penrose have recently come forward with a range of ingenious theories. All purport to explain, in one way or another, consciousness as an epiphenomenon of physical and chemical processes taking place in the brain—and all fail utterly. They fail not because their models are insufficiently accurate or detailed, but because they are trying to do what is, from the outset, impossible.[37] The truth is that no account of what goes on at the mechanistic level of the brain can shed any light whatsoever on why consciousness exists. No theory can explain why the brain shouldn't work exactly as it does, yet without giving rise to the feeling we all have of "what it is like to be." And there is, I believe, a very simple reason for this. The brain does not produce consciousness at all, any more than a television set creates the programs that appear on its screen. On the contrary, the brain filters and restricts consciousness, just as our senses limit the totality of experience to which we might otherwise have access.[38]

Cognitive scientist Donald D. Hoffman, mentioned above, offers a similar explanation of the failure of physicalists to explain how matter could give rise to consciousness:

> The scientific study of consciousness is in the embarrassing position of having no scientific theory of consciousness. I believe that consciousness and its contents are all that exists. Space-time, matter and fields never were the fundamental denizens of the universe but have always been, from their beginning, among the humbler contents of consciousness, dependent on it for their very being. . . . If this is right, if consciousness is fundamental, then we should not be surprised that, despite centuries of effort by the most brilliant of minds, there is as yet no physicalist theory of consciousness, no theory that explains how mindless matter or energy or fields could be, or cause, conscious experience.[39]

Despite this failure, the physicalist view inspires rapturous, messianic, triumphal confidence in its adherents, who ardently strive to extend the physicalist caliphate into every nook and cranny of the life sciences. Their zeal can be unbounded. For example, philosopher Dennett is reported as saying that he would commit suicide if paranormal phenomena turn out to be real.[40]

The implication that there might be room in science for a spiritual component is met with derision. Special contempt is reserved for the possibility that humans might survive bodily death, for this would be the death knell for the mind-equals-brain assumption on which physicalism rests. Therefore, the extinction of consciousness with brain death must be total; no variety of survival can be contemplated. This is particularly obvious when physicalists themselves have near-death experiences suggesting survival following physical death. When they describe these experiences publicly, they have been bullied by their physicalist colleagues into publicly retracting any implication that something might survive the death of the body.[41]

Many physicalists consider the idea of surviving bodily death so dangerous that it must be put down at all costs. These efforts can lead to a deliberate cover-up that masquerades as an effort to protect science. Harvard psychologist William James reported that a leading biologist once told him:

> Even if such a thing were true, scientists ought to band together to keep it suppressed and concealed. It would undo the uniformity of Nature and all sorts of other things without which scientists cannot carry on their pursuits.[42]

Physicalists often maintain that they actually prefer annihilation with physical death to any sort of survival. Longing for immortality is seen as a defect of character or a philosophical sellout in people too weak-willed to face their impending doom. In the face of certain extermination, one should simply man-up and go quietly, proudly, and bravely into that dark night. There is a hint of this heroic martyrdom in Lord Bertrand Russell's famous comment: "I believe that when I die I shall rot, and nothing of my ego will survive. . . . I should scorn to shiver with terror at the thought of annihilation."[43]

Human Costs

[S]cience has gone too far in breaking down man's belief in his spiritual greatness... and has given him the belief that he is merely an insignificant animal that has arisen by chance and necessity in an insignificant planet lost in the great cosmic immensity. . . . The principal trouble with mankind today is that the intellectual leaders are too arrogant in their self-sufficiency. We must realize the great unknowns in the material makeup and operation of our brains, in the relationship of brain to mind, in our creative imagination, and in the uniqueness of the psyche. When we think of these unknowns as well as the unknown of how we come to be in the first place, we should be much more humble.[44]

—Sir John Eccles

Physicalism comes with enormous human costs, which, I believe, are vastly underestimated by its proponents. Total annihilation is an inescapable part of the physicalism doctrine. Carl G. Jung, the Swiss psychiatrist, said, "The decisive question for man is: Is he related to something infinite or not? That is the telling question of his life."[45] If consciousness is produced by the brain and vanishes with physical death, as physicalists insist, then any meaningful relationship to "something infinite" is a chimera. Novelist George Orwell was among those who decried the impact of this morbid outlook, saying, "The major problem of our time is the decay of belief in personal immortality."[46] Jung felt so strongly about this issue that he made it a principle in his patients' therapy. "As a doctor," he said, "I make every effort to strengthen the belief in immortality. . . ."[47]

One's view of immortality depends on one's concept of time; yet, there is no agreed-on definition of time in modern physics. As Nobel Prize–winning physicist Richard Feynman acknowledged, "What is time? We physicists work with it every day, but don't ask me what it is. It's just too difficult to think about."[48] The philosopher Ludwig Wittgenstein saw the relevance of the "time question" to immortality, saying, "If we take eternity to mean not infinite temporal duration but timelessness, then eternal life belongs to those who live in the present."[49] Because of the unsettled definition of time in modern physics, physicalists might at least acknowledge that while modern physics does not affirm immortality, it does not exclude it, either. But this acknowledgment is seldom met.

The belief in immortality has helped sustain human hope for perhaps the entire span of human history. The human cost of a failure of this belief is not admitted within physicalism. The public stance of many physicalists, as mentioned, is to keep a stiff upper lip, flex one's intellectual muscle, and deny any desire or need for such a frivolous belief. Yet the old channels within the psyche run deep, and merely declaring immortality undesirable or unnecessary does not make it so.[50]

The fear of death is humanity's Great Disease, the terror that has caused more suffering throughout history than all the physical diseases combined. As Ernest Becker said in his Pulitzer Prize–winning book *The Denial of Death*, "[T]he idea of death, the fear of it, haunts the human animal like nothing else; it is the mainspring of human activity—activity designed largely to avoid the fatality of death, to overcome it by denying in some way that it is the final destiny for man."[51]

The physicalists' certainty—that these issues are settled and the verdict is in; that materialism reigns; that spirituality and any form of survival are self-delusions—is regarded as overheated swagger by many consciousness researchers. Edward F. Kelly, speaking for his colleagues, states:

> We believe it takes astonishing hubris to dismiss
> *en masse* the collective experience of a large pro-
> portion of our forebears, including persons widely
> recognized as pillars of all human civilization,
> and we are united in believing that the single most
> important task confronting all of modernity is
> that of *meaningful* reconciliation of science and
> religion. . . . [W]e believe that emerging develop-
> ments within science itself are leading inexorably
> in the direction of an expanded scientific under-
> standing of nature, one that can accommodate
> realities of a "spiritual" sort . . . .[52]

PRACTICALITY

But not *just* of a spiritual sort. For instance, eminent quantum theorist Henry P. Stapp has expressed concern about the impact of the physicalistic views on the nitty-gritty, practical ways in which we free-range humans live our lives. In his paper "Attention, Intention, and Will in Quantum Physics," he stated, "It has become now widely appreciated that assimilation by the general public of this 'scientific' view, according to which each human is basically a mechanical robot, is likely to have a significant and corrosive impact on the moral fabric of society."[53] Stapp also warned of the "growing tendency of people to exonerate themselves by arguing that it is not 'I' who is at fault, but some mechanical process within: 'my genes made me do it'; or 'my high blood-sugar content made me do it.'"[54] (The acclaimed science writer Margaret Wertheim calls this the "Genes-R-Us" view.)[55] Stapp shows how hard-core physicalism lets us off the hook by assuming that the world unfolds on its own, according to the alleged meaningless laws of nature. We are not active participants in such a process, but passive observers at best and victims at worst.

Cosmologist and quantum physicist Menas C. Kafatos, of California's Chapman University, is the co-author (with Robert Nadeau) of *The Conscious Universe: Parts and Wholes in Physical Reality*.[56] Like Stapp, he is concerned with the practical importance of consciousness in daily life, what our future will look like, and whether we shall have a future that can support life as we know it. He writes:

Are these issues yet another set of intellectual arguments that scientists, philosophers and academics make? They are very relevant to your life and your healthy living: We seem to be bound by our minds, often giving us no peace. Yet, if what we view as reality is really the product of the mind, then we can approach our mind as a tool, as a friendly tool, get it on "our side," so to speak . . . [for] healthy living . . . what we should pass on to the next generations.[57]

Your Spouse as a Differential Equation

Stapp's concern that physicalistic science defines us as mechanical robots is a grave issue. If we peel back the layers of physicalistic logic behind the robotic view, what do we find? We come face-to-face with serious illogic, which philosopher of science Sir Karl Popper describes in his 1965 Compton Lecture.[58] Popper observed that, according to physicalistic determinism, mental states are the result of

> . . . a certain physical structure of the holder—perhaps of his brain. Accordingly, we are deceiving ourselves whenever we believe that there are such things as *arguments* or *reasons* which make us accept determinism. Purely physical conditions including our physical environment make us say or accept whatever we say or accept.[59]

Popper called the physicalistic narrative "promissory materialism"—the notion that one day, not so very long from now, we'll be able to give a completely physical account of consciousness. Popper predicted that, lured by periodic advances in brain science, "we shall be talking less and less about experiences, perceptions, thoughts, beliefs, purposes and aims; and more and more about brain processes.. . . ."[60] His prediction has come to pass.

Sir John Eccles agreed with Popper. He excoriated the physicalist narrative, saying:

> [P]romissory materialism [is] a superstition without a rational foundation. The more we discover about the brain, the more clearly do we distinguish between the brain events and the mental phenomena, and the more wonderful do both the brain events and the mental phenomena become. Promissory materialism is simply a religious belief held by dogmatic materialists . . . who confuse their religion with their science. It has all the features of a messianic prophecy . . . .[61]

Because physicalists maintain that no one is immune from physical laws, the implication is that everyone is a mechanical robot, including, inevitably, physicalists themselves. As Eccles observed, this leads to an "effective *reductio ad absurdum*."[62] Why absurd? Consider Dennett's earlier observation that free will is an illusion. In asserting such, he presumably believes he was using his own free will to arrive at the conclusion that free will does not exist. But physicalists never acknowledge this pretzel-like contradiction in their "logic." Determined, robotic behavior is for others. The robotic strictures of physicalism do not apply to them. Thus they behave as if *their* conclusions are freely arrived at and should be taken seriously. They *must* exempt themselves from their physicalistic theory, for if they did not they would have no claim to truth, no compelling "arguments or reasons," as Popper noted. They cannot acknowledge that, if physicalism is valid, they arrived at their conclusions *not* as a result of freely considered data, but because their atoms, molecules and brain made them do so. They are thus hoisted by their own petard.

This ludicrous situation was parodied by Sir Arthur Eddington in his 1927 Gifford Lecture:

> The materialist who is convinced that all phenomena arise from electrons and quanta and the like controlled by mathematical formulae, must presumably hold the belief that his wife is a rather elaborate differential equation, but he is probably tactful enough not to obtrude this opinion into domestic life.[63]

Futurist Willis Harman identified the hypocrisy of the physicalist position:

> Science for three and a half centuries has been built
> on the premise that consciousness as a causal fac-
> tor does not have to be included. . . . [But] nobody
> has ever lived life on the basis of such a contrary
> premise. Nobody has ever said, "I'm going to live
> my life as though my consciousness—my mind—
> weren't capable of making decisions, making
> choices, taking action. . . ."[64]

In the same vein, philosopher Alfred North Whitehead
wryly stated, "Scientists, animated by the purpose of prov-
ing they are purposeless, constitute an interesting subject for
study."[65] Sir John Eccles concurred:

> In the protected duchies of academic philosophy
> and psychology . . . professional philosophers and
> psychologists think up the notion that there are no
> thoughts, come to believe that there are no beliefs,
> and feel strongly that there are no feelings.[66]

He observed that if future generations ever erect a Hall of
Human Silliness, biological determinism—the idea that we are
totally controlled by our atoms, DNA, and genes—will occupy
a position of high honor.

EVIDENCE

The evidence favoring a view of consciousness that transcends
physicalism is enormous and is too vast to be described here.

Several excellent summaries have recently appeared, such as *Varieties of Anomalous Experience: Examining the Scientific Evidence*[67]; *Irreducible Mind: Toward a Psychology for the 21st Century*[68]; *Beyond Physicalism: Toward Reconciliation of Science and Spirituality*, as mentioned; and consciousness researcher Dean Radin's *The Conscious Universe*[69] and *Entangled Minds*.[70]

All told, the evidence from more than a century of consciousness research shows that consciousness can do things brains cannot do. Thousands of studies show that humans can psychically *insert* information *into* the environment nonlocally, and also psychically *acquire* information *from* the environment nonlocally.

What does "nonlocal" imply? If you have ever shared thoughts or physical sensations with someone at a distance, or knew or dreamed about something before it happened, or experienced something that could not be explained by the use of your physical senses, you *may* have had a taste of what "nonlocal" means, or at least a glimpse of what nonlocal events *can* look like. I say "may" and "can" because we can deceive ourselves, so we must be careful in how we interpret any experience in life.

Nonlocality is a concept that physicists apply to a class of events whose description relates to the speed of light.[71] As physicist Nick Herbert explains, "A nonlocal connection links up one location with another without crossing space, without decay, and without delay." These connections have three identifying characteristics, says Herbert. They are *unmediated* (no connecting signal is involved), *unmitigated* (the strength of the correlations does not fade with increasing distance), and *immediate* (they are instantaneous).[72]

Nonlocality is subdivided by some physicists into three types. Type 1 is spatial nonlocality; Type 2 is temporal nonlocality; and Type 3 nonlocality is both spatial and temporal.[73]

But physics does not own nonlocality, and physicists do not have a monopoly on nonlocal events or the language that describes them. People were routinely having nonlocal experiences millennia before quantum physics was discovered in the twentieth century. We are not obligated to cede the phenomenon of nonlocality to scientists who have chosen to nuance the term differently and may have little understanding of nonlocal human experiences.

The potential relevance of nonlocality to consciousness is expressed by historian of religions Huston Smith: "[I]f nonlocality holds for the material world, what about the world of the human mind? If both mind and matter are nonlocal, we are on our way to regaining what was lost in Newton's time—a complete, whole world in which we can live complete, whole lives, in the awareness that we are more interrelated than we had thought."[74]

There are compelling scientific, historic, and experiential reasons for believing that consciousness behaves nonlocally in space and time, that it is spatially unconfinable to brains and bodies, and that it is temporally unconfinable to the present. The evidence suggests that space and time are simply not applicable to certain operations of consciousness.[75] This evidence overwhelmingly suggests that consciousness is both trans-spatial and trans-temporal, that it is *not in* space and time.[76] Empirical evidence shows that brains are separate, but minds are not. In the domain of mind and consciousness, separation is not fundamental. The degree of spatial separation of individual minds, the distance involved, is not important, and the connections are instantaneous or immediate, whether the humans involved are an inch apart, on opposite sides of the planet or even presumably the universe.

Many individuals accept the evidence that minds might operate at a distance, but they rebel at the possibility that minds might function outside the present. Yet, scores of experiments indicate that human consciousness can operate nonlocally not only in space but also in time. Temporal nonlocality of consciousness has been solidly demonstrated. In these studies, intentions appear to influence certain types of events in the past, even though they are presumed to have already happened.[77] In addition, individuals also appear capable of acquiring accurate information from the future before it has occurred, especially if this information is of an unpleasant or traumatic nature.[78] The nonlocal picture of consciousness that has emerged from these studies, in which separation of minds is not fundamental in space or time, has enormous implications. A consciousness that is nonlocal with respect to space is *infinite* and *omnipresent*. A consciousness that is nonlocal with respect to time is *eternal* and *immortal*. And if individual consciousnesses are boundless and boundaryless, at some level they must come together to form a whole—a Universal or One Mind. *When we therefore describe* consciousness as eternal, infinite, and one, we are not speaking symbolically, metaphorically or poetically. We are invoking empirical science, in addition to human experience.

THE SQUARE ROOT OF A SONNET

[We] must boldly take an anti-mechanistic and pluralistic stand on the nature of science. It is almost comically arrogant to think that Nature should conform to our favorite modes of investigation, or that we should dictate to Nature the forms in which we are willing to accept its secrets. . . .

The real trailblazers . . . will be those who break from the rigid and fruitless tradition of looking for analyses of [human] capacities in terms of lower-level processes and mechanisms. . . . [We] must repudiate the idea that only the methods of physics yield genuine understanding . . . .[79]

—STEPHEN E. BRAUDE

Physicalists object, claiming that these nonlocal, consciousness-related phenomena cannot possibly be true; if they were valid, they would violate the so-called iron-clad laws of nature, which is unthinkable. Sir Arthur Eddington forcefully rejected this line of reasoning in his 1929 Swarthmore Lecture: "Materialism in its literal sense is long sense dead." Noting that the material stuff of the world has been replaced by mathematical symbols and equations, he cautioned, "You cannot apply such a scheme to the parts of your personality which are not measurable by symbols any more than you can extract the square root of a sonnet." Natural law, he insisted, is therefore not applicable to the "unseen world" of consciousness.[80] What is being violated by the events in question is not the laws of nature, but the stubborn prejudices of the physicalists.

Physics has evolved considerably since Eddington's observations in 1929. Are his opinions relevant today? I suggest they are even more relevant. Many outstanding scientists have stipulated that nonlocal, consciousness-related events are fully compatible with emerging concepts within contemporary physics. For example, the eminent physicist Olivier Costa de Beauregard observed, "Today's physics allows for the existence of 'paranormal' phenomena of telepathy, precognition, and psychokinesis. . . . The whole concept of 'nonlocality' in contemporary physics requires this possibility."[81] And, "Far from being 'irrational,' *the paranormal is postulated by today's physics*" (emphasis in original).[82] George Wald, a Nobel laureate in biology, stated, "Mind, rather than emerging as a late outgrowth in the evolution of life, has existed always . . . the source and condition of physical reality."[83] And, "I do not need spiritual enlightenment to know that I am one with the universe. That is just good physics."[84]

Henry P. Stapp has stated, "The new physics presents *prima facie* evidence that our human thoughts are linked to nature by nonlocal connections: what a person chooses to do in one region seems immediately to affect what is true elsewhere in the universe. . . . [O]ur thoughts . . . *do* something" (emphasis in original).[85] Gerald Feinberg, the respected Columbia University physicist, concurred: "If [so-called paranormal events] indeed occur, no change in the fundamental equations of physics would be needed to describe them."[86] Henry Margenau, the esteemed Yale University physicist and member of Princeton University's Institute for Advanced Study, agreed. Speaking of so-called paranormal events, he said, "Strangely, it does not seem possible to find the scientific laws or principles violated by the existence of [these phenomena]. We can find contradictions between [their occurrence] and our culturally accepted view of reality—but not—as many of us have believed—between [their occurrence] and the scientific laws that have been so laboriously developed."[87]

One of the great breakthroughs in physics in recent years is the discovery that nonlocal connections and entanglement—nonlocality's close cousin—are now known to occur in the macroscopic, biological, human domain, as well as in the invisible, microscopic, subatomic realm. For materialists who have long denied this possibility, this can be a shocking realization. As physicist Vlatko Vedral emphasized in a groundbreaking article in *Scientific American* in 2011:

> Quantum mechanics is commonly said to be a theory of microscopic things: molecules, atoms, subatomic particles. . . . [T]his convenient partitioning of the world is a myth. . . . It is but a useful approximation of a world that is quantum at all scales. . . . Over the past several years experimentalists

have seen quantum effects in a growing number of macroscopic systems. *The quintessential quantum effect, entanglement, can occur in large systems as well as warm ones—including living organisms. . . .* Until the past decade, experimentalists had not confirmed that quantum behavior persists on a macroscopic scale. Today, however, they routinely do. These effects are more pervasive than anyone ever suspected. They may operate in the cells of our body. . . . We can't simply write [quantum effects] off as mere details that matter only on the very smallest scales. . . . *The entanglements are primary* [emphasis added].[88]

Rather than being contrary to nature, as physicalists insist, distant, nonlocal, entangled connections in and between living creatures might be *expected* to develop, because they would convey a survival advantage to the individual possessing them. As physicist Johann Summhammer of the Vienna University of Technology has stated:

Entanglement would lead to a Darwinian advantage: Entanglement could coordinate biochemical reactions in different parts of a cell, or in different parts of an organ. It could allow correlated firings of distant neurons. . . . [and] coordinate the behaviors of members of a species, because it is independent of distance and requires no physical link. It is also conceivable that entanglement correlates processes between members of different species, and even between living systems and the inanimate world.[89]

Human-level, nonlocal, entangled events between individuals, often called parapsychological, paranormal, or psi happenings, appear to demonstrate the three essential characteristics of nonlocal subatomic events mentioned above: they appear to be unmediated, unmitigated, and immediate. Some consciousness researchers do not believe these similarities are accidental or trivial, but reveal fundamental, intrinsic relationships between consciousness and the quantum domain. As Dean Radin states, "I propose that psi is the human experience of the [quantum-]entangled universe. . . . [T]he ontological parallels implied by [quantum] entanglement and psi are so compelling that I believe they'd be foolish to ignore."[90] I agree. But, as yet, there is no conclusive evidence that subatomic nonlocality or entanglement necessarily explains, underlies, or causes the nonlocality of mind or consciousness. Despite the parallels, we may be dealing only with correspondences in terminology—or not; further investigation will tell. In the meantime, we should acknowledge the possibility suggested by Radin and others, because the parallels are profound.

The depth of this empirical evidence may surprise many. There are at least six areas in consciousness research which resoundingly demonstrate the nonlocal, beyond-the-brain actions of consciousness. Experiments in these areas have been replicated repeatedly in labs around the world, each area giving odds against chance of around a billion to one, or combined odds against chance of 10^{54} to one, a truly astronomical number. These areas of research, too extensive to be reviewed here, are remote viewing, random number generator influence, Ganzfeld, the Global Consciousness Project, presentiment, and precognition.[91]

This evidence is not a cosmetic reworking of current materialistic views, but a radical departure or paradigm shift in current thinking. Edward F. Kelly summarizes what is at stake:

> [This emerging world picture] is not just the same old physicalistic world with an altered expression, but a world whose constitution is fundamentally different in ways that matter to us human beings. [This] vision . . . provides an antidote to the prevailing postmodern disenchantment of the world and demeaning of human possibilities. It not only more accurately and fully describes our human condition but engenders hope and encourages human flourishing. It provides reasons for us to believe that freedom is real, that our human choices matter, and that we have barely scratched the surface of our human potentials. It also addresses the urgent need for a greater sense

of worldwide community and interdependence, a sustainable *ethos*, by demonstrating that under the surface we and the world are much more extensively interconnected than previously realized. We strongly suspect that our individual and collective fates in these exceptionally dangerous and difficult times—indeed, the fate of our precious planet and *all* of its passengers—may ultimately hinge upon wider recognition and more effective utilization of the higher states of being that are potentially available to us but largely ignored or even actively suppressed by our post-modern civilization with its strange combination of self-aggrandizing individualism and fundamentalist tribalisms (emphasis in original).[92]

THEORY

One of the main obstacles to the penetration of this evidence into mainstream science is the lack of a generally accepted theory of how these nonlocal, so-called paranormal, phenomena *could* be true. But if this is a weakness for consciousness research, it is equally problematic for mind-equals-brain physicalism, which is wanting of any successful explanatory theory of consciousness, as mentioned.

The basic conundrum is *not* how a particular so-called paranormal event—telepathy, clairvoyance, precognition, psychokinesis, or the survival of bodily death—could be valid, but how we can consciously be aware of *ordinary* experiences. In other words, the primary mystery is the very existence of consciousness. We breezily ignore the role of consciousness in the mundane events of our lives: how we decide what to have for dinner; how we choose to raise a fork of spaghetti while opening our mouth and swallowing soon thereafter; how we can experience the redness of the sauce, the taste of the garlic, the satisfaction of a lovely presentation, the bouquet of the wine, and admiration for the chef. These feats are beyond the ability of the most sophisticated robot. Although physicalists offer a flurry of explanations in sensorimotor terms for these accomplishments, their explanations are empty of the crucial role of consciousness in all such sequences.

Any experience in which consciousness is involved is mysterious, whether deciphering the Lorenz Equations or deciding to pick our nose. Commonplace events are as enigmatic as any of the so-called paranormal pyrotechnics that provoke incredulity and objections from physicalists. There are not two categories of consciousness-related phenomena, normal and paranormal. They are *all* "para"—or "normal," as the case may be. If we were sufficiently awake, we might realize that the lifting of a finger or the experience of love is as astonishing as the survival of bodily death. When physicalists bridle at the extraordinary and ignore the commonplace, in biblical imagery they are "straining at a gnat and swallowing a camel."[93]

Voltaire—no friend of spirituality—realized this. He observed, "It is not more surprising to be born twice than once."[94] He understood that the marvel is life and consciousness, not how many turns they make on the wheel of existence.

DOUBLE DAZZLEMENT

"To live is so startling it leaves little time for anything else," exulted Emily Dickinson.[95] And physician-researcher-essayist Lewis Thomas (1913–1993) observed, "Statistically, the probability of any one of us being here is so small that you'd think the mere fact of existing would keep us in a contented dazzlement of surprise."[96] Add to this the fact that we are not only here but conscious as well, and you'd think we might experience a state of double dazzlement. But no; for most people, most of the time, consciousness is so ordinary and boring it largely escapes notice: the height of cosmic ingratitude.

Awakening us to conscious awareness of the ordinary is the calling of every great poet and artist. This is the point of Tennyson's humble "Flower in the Crannied Wall," in which he said: ". . . *if* I could understand/What you are, root and all, and all in all,/I should know what God and man is."[97] And as George Eliot wrote in *Middlemarch*, "If we had a keen vision of all that is ordinary in human life, it would be like hearing the grass grow or the squirrel's heart beat, and we should die of that roar which is the other side of silence." But Eliot felt compelled to add, "As it is, the quickest of us walk about well wadded with stupidity. . . . We do not expect people to be deeply moved by what is not unusual."[98]

If our well-waddedness prevents us from recognizing the extraordinariness of the ordinary, or acknowledging extraordinary experiences, how do we strip away the cognitive padding that insulates us from this awareness? This is a crucial question, because dedicated physicalists typically avoid evidence that contradicts their assumptions. As one such individual commented about nonlocal experiences, "This is the sort of thing I would not believe, even if it really happened."[99] Many consciousness researchers have written extensively about how to openly approach and experience the evidence for a nonphysicalist view. In fact, the overall thrust of all the five works mentioned above, and hundreds more that could be mentioned, is to nudge us into fuller awareness through an enlarged conceptual framework, as well as through experiences such as contemplative practices, a meditative walk in the woods, or paying attention to a baby's laugh. But what must be continually emphasized is that *the evidence for a nonmaterial, nonphysical view of consciousness is also solidly empirical, and not just subjective and experiential: experience* and *experiment.*

Jumbo Shrimp

The incompleteness of contemporary science regarding consciousness is particularly obvious in the blank spots that have arisen on our current maps of the universe. Edward F. Kelly and David E. Presti note:

> [D]espite all of our genuine scientific knowledge
> and technical expertise, patiently accumulated
> over centuries of systematic and disciplined effort,
> we . . . apparently overlooked until the past decade
> or so something like 95% of the *physical* content
> of the universe—its so-called dark matter and
> energy. This chastening discovery should certainly
> encourage humility, and perhaps a sense of excite-
> ment as well, regarding what may remain to be
> discovered about the human mind![100]

Because physicalists assume that extraordinary, anomalous, consciousness-related phenomena cannot exist in principle, they generally refuse to examine the overall evidence for
these happenings. In so doing, they may have duplicated the
failure of astrophysicists and cosmologists to notice ninety-five
percent of the matter and energy in the universe; except in this
case the overlooked item is the fundamental nature of consciousness and its nonlocal manifestations.

Suppose I said to you, "I would like to be your internal medicine physician, but you should know that I understand nothing about ninety-five percent of the organs in your
body." You would probably be disgusted by my audacity and
turn away, as you should. Should we not react with equal cau-
tion to physicalists who want to be our interpreters of reality,
when they are in the dark regarding ninety-five percent of the
physical content of the universe? With such massive lacunae

regarding physical issues, why trust them when consciousness is concerned?

Why do entities such as consciousness remain invisible to physicalists? David Darling observes, "If science searches the universe—as it does—for certain kinds of truth, then these are inevitably the only ones it will find. Everything else will slip through the net."[101] The net used by consciousness researchers is made of finer mesh than the net employed by physicalists; it captures facts and phenomena physicalists never notice.

There is no room for smugness, however, because this short-coming—the failure to notice—affects everyone in one way or another, as novelist Stephen King humorously points out:

> [J]umbo shrimp, everybody's oxymoron. They're the big shrimp that nobody ate in restaurants until 1955 or 1960 because, until then, nobody thought of going shrimping after dark. They were there all the time, living their prosaic shrimp lives, but nobody caught them. So when they finally caught them it was, "Hello! Look at this. This is something entirely new." And if the shrimp could talk they'd say, "[W]e're not new. We've been around for a couple of thousand years. You were just too dumb to look for us."[102]

Noticing: how simple! Yet, as the folk saying goes, "If you want to hide the treasure, put it in plain sight." This is nowhere truer than with consciousness, our quarry. How could something as ordinary as consciousness be a treasure? Our insensitivity is why the great disciplines of awareness strive to yank us out of our slumber and return us to the simple act of noticing. Lawrence LeShan, the great psychologist and consciousness researcher, defines meditation as the art of "doing one thing well."[103] Doing one thing well requires undiluted attention, awareness, noticing —including the fact that we are, against all odds, mysteriously, gloriously, wondrously, *conscious*. Thus poet Mary Oliver's "instructions for living a life": "Pay attention./Be astonished./Tell about it."[104]

MIND AT LARGE

The individual mind is immanent but not only in the body. It is immanent also in pathways and messages outside the body; and there is a larger Mind of which the individual mind is only a sub-system. This larger Mind is comparable to God and is perhaps what some people mean by "God," but it is still immanent in the total interconnected social system and planetary ecology.[105]

—GREGORY BATESON, *Steps to an Ecology of Mind*

A recurring theme of modern consciousness research is that there is a larger, more extensive consciousness beyond our individual mind, which unites all individuals in a shared existence. This view can be traced back for at least three millennia, appearing in various forms in Eastern traditions. But this concept is also threaded through Western philosophies. Plato said, "[H]uman nature was originally One and we were a whole."[106] Hippocrates stated, "There is one common flow, one common breathing, all things are in sympathy." A millennium later, the Renaissance philosopher Pico della Mirandola believed that the world is governed by a "unity whereby one creature is united with the others and all parts of the world constitute one world."[107] In the nineteenth century, the German philosopher G. W. F. Hegel called distant mental exchanges between humans the "magic tie." He believed that "the intuitive spirit oversteps the confines of time and space; it beholds things remote; things long past, and things to come."[108] Arthur Schopenhauer, also in nineteenth-century Germany, suggested that a single event could figure in two or more different chains of circumstance, linking the fates of different individuals in profound ways. He believed in a form of communication that took place between humans during dreams.[109] And as Walt Whitman, America's bard, proclaimed, "All these separations and gaps shall be taken up and hook'd and link'd together. . . . Nature and Man shall be disjoin'd and diffused no more. . . ."[110]

A particularly eloquent proponent of this collective, transindividual view of consciousness was the British classicist and psychical researcher Frederic W. H. Myers, who wrote:

> There exists a more comprehensive consciousness, a profounder faculty, which for the most part

remains potential only . . . but from which the consciousness and the faculty of earth-life are mere selections. . . . [N]o Self of which we can here have cognizance is in reality more than a fragment of a larger Self—revealed in a fashion at once shifting and limited through an organism not so framed as to afford it full manifestation.[111]

It is little known that many prominent architects of twentieth-century science have also affirmed a unified, collective aspect of consciousness, in which all individual minds are connected as a single whole. As Erwin Schrödinger put it:

To divide or multiply consciousness is something meaningless. In all the world, there is no kind of framework within which we can find consciousness in the plural; this is simply something we construct because of the spatio-temporal plurality of individuals, but it is a false construction. . . . The category of *number*, of *whole* and of *parts* are then simply not applicable to it.[112]

. . . The overall number of minds is just one. . . . In truth there is only one mind.[113]

[I]nconceivable as it seems to ordinary reason, you—and all other conscious beings as such—are

all in all. Hence this life of yours which you are
living is not merely a piece of the entire existence,
but is in a certain sense the *whole*; only this whole
is not so constituted that it can be surveyed in one
single glance.[114]

Sir Arthur Eddington agreed about the unitary nature of
consciousness: "The idea of a universal Mind or Logos would
be, I think, a fairly plausible inference from the present state
of scientific theory; at least it is in harmony with it."[115] David
Bohm also observed, "Deep down the consciousness of mankind is one. This is a virtual certainty . . . and if we don't see
this it's because we are blinding ourselves to it."[116] Bohm and
his colleague Basil Hiley further stated, "The notion of a separate organism is clearly an abstraction, as is also its boundary.
Underlying all this is unbroken wholeness even though our civilization has developed in such a way as to strongly emphasize
the separation into parts."[117] From the poet's perspective, William Butler Yeats agreed:

1. That the borders of our minds are ever shifting, and that many minds can flow into one
   another, as it were, and create or reveal a single
   mind, a single energy.

2. That the borders of our memories are as shifting,
   and that our memories are a part of one great
   memory, the memory of Nature herself.[118]

These images are congruent with Jung's concept of the collective unconscious, Emerson's Over-Soul, and Aldous Huxley's Mind at Large—a Universal or One Mind, a plenum that fuels our experience as individual sentient, conscious creatures. As philosopher Michael Grosso has stated, "Our individual minds are surface growths that appear separate and distinct but whose roots lie in a deeper psychic underground; there we are mutually entangled and part of a more extended mental system."[119]

A common objection to this view is the horror of being swallowed up and homogenized in a cosmic blob of undifferentiated consciousness, in which individuality disappears. This concern is emphatically rejected by those who claim to have experienced the larger connections. William James emphasized that a sense of individuality is preserved, not extinguished, in the Universal or One Mind:

> We with our lives are like islands in the sea, or like trees in the forest. The maple and the pine may whisper to each other with their leaves . . . [but] the trees also commingle their roots in the darkness underground, and the islands also hang together through the ocean's bottom. Just so there is a continuum of cosmic consciousness, against which our individuality builds but accidental fences, and into which our several minds plunge as into a mother-sea or reservoir. Our "normal" consciousness is circumscribed for adaptation to our external earthly environment, but the fence is

weak in spots, and fitful influences from beyond leak in, showing the otherwise unverifiable common connection.[120]

THE BRAIN AS FILTER: THE MEASLY TRICKLE

The brain does not generate thought . . . any more than the wire generates electric current.[121]

—PAUL BRUNTON

A concept related to mind-at-large is that the brain operates not as a generator or producer of mind or consciousness, but as a *filter* that receives, limits, transforms, and transmits information that arises external to the brain. This reducing function is vital; otherwise we would likely be overwhelmed by informational input, which would compromise our ability to get on successfully in the world. An impressive array of historical, philosophical and scientific opinion has accumulated in favor of the brain-as-filter view, including Aldous Huxley, F. W. H. Myers, William James, Henri Bergson, F. C. S. Schiller, C. D. Broad, and many others.

We pay a price for this stepped-down version of consciousness, however. An experience of our essential nature is obscured. Aldous Huxley describes the dilemma:

[E]ach one of us is potentially Mind at Large. But in so far as we are animals, our business at all costs is to survive. To make biological survival possible, Mind at Large has to be funneled through the reducing valve of the brain and nervous system. What comes out at the other end is a measly trickle of the kind of consciousness which will help us to stay alive on the surface of this particular planet.[122]

Or, as David Darling has said, we are conscious not because of the brain, but in spite of it.[123]

Michael Grosso summarizes the key features of this view:

The brain *transmits*—it does not *produce*—consciousness. . . . [M]ind is not a property of the brain but a user of the brain. . . . Consciousness preexists the brain; it does not emerge from the brain. There is a *transpersonal* mind, i.e., a mind at large, a cosmic consciousness, James's "mother-sea" of consciousness. . . . [There is an] ever-fluctuating threshold that separates subliminal from supraliminal mental life.[124]

In his book *Soulmaking*, Grosso uses the radio analogy:

A crude analysis with radio and radio waves: the radio does not produce the radio waves; it detects, transmits, and filters them. If your radio breaks

> down, it doesn't follow that the sounds you're lis-
> tening to have ceased to exist. They just cease to
> be detectable. An analogy is possible between this
> and the mind-brain relationship.[125]

The permeability of our mental filter is not fixed. Filters can become clogged or they can become more efficient, so that the "measly trickle" is increased in quantity or quality. An analogy is desalination devices, which filter out salt in favor of pure, life-sustaining water. As a consequence of this "ever-fluctuating threshold," experiences such as telepathy, clairvoyance, precognition, and extraordinary knowing may occur. Throughout human history, techniques have been developed to alter this threshold in favor of expanded awareness, as in various mystical, religious, spiritual, and native traditions.

CREATIVITY

The "cash value" of the beyond-the-brain models of mind-matter interaction can be seen in the domain of creativity. Physicalistic models of brain function fail to explain, for example, the mind-boggling feats of savants, who are commonly mentally impaired, or the genius of prodigies such as the great mathematician Srinivasa Ramanujan.[126] But if all individual minds are connected with one another and to a domain of consciousness that transcends ordinary awareness, and if the threshold between expanded and contracted awareness is continually shifting, individuals might have occasional access to all conceivable knowledge, past, present, and future. This may account for what F. W. H. Myers called a "subliminal uprush" of genius-level creativity and understanding.[127]

These "uprushes" can be spectacular when they occur in children. Developmental psychologist Joseph Chilton Pearce reports a striking example. When he was in his early thirties, teaching humanities in a college, he was engrossed in theology and the psychology of Carl Jung. Pearce describes himself as "obsessed" by the nature of the God-human relationship, and his reading on the subject was extensive. One morning as he was preparing for an early class, his five-year-old son came into his room, sat down on the edge of the bed, and launched into a twenty-minute discourse on the nature of God and man. Pearce was astonished. He states:

> He spoke in perfect, publishable sentences, without pause or haste, and in a flat monotone. He used complex theological terminology and told me, it seemed, everything there was to know. As I listened, astonished, the hair rose on my neck; I felt goose bumps, and, finally, tears streamed down my face. I was in the midst of the uncanny, the inexplicable. My son's ride to kindergarten arrived, horn blowing, and he got up and left. I was unnerved and arrived late to my class. What I had heard was awesome, but too vast and far beyond any concept I had had to that point. The gap was so

> great I could remember almost no details and lit-
> tle of the broad panorama he had presented. . . . He
> wasn't picking up his materials from me. I hadn't
> acquired anything like what he described and
> would, in fact, be in my mid-fifties and involved in
> meditation before I did. . . . My son had no recol-
> lection of the event.[128]

Many consciousness researchers recognize that there are deeper ways of knowing than the rational, logical, and analytical methods usually attributed to "doing science." These deeper ways do not deny the physical senses and reason, but they include and transcend them. We get glimpses of this process from exemplars who have employed them, such as Thomas Edison, America's great inventor, who stated:

> People say I have created things. I have never cre-
> ated anything. I get impressions from the Uni-
> verse at large and work them out, but I am only a
> plate on a record or a receiving apparatus—what
> you will. Thoughts are really impressions that we
> get from outside.[129]

Logic, reason, and intellectual analysis take a back seat in this unfolding. As Eugene Wigner put it, "The discovery of the laws of nature requires first and foremost intuition, conceiving of a picture and a great many subconscious processes.

The . . . confirmation of these laws is another matter. . . . [L]ogic comes after intuition."[130] Baron Carl Friedrich von Weizsäecker, renowned physicist and a student of Werner Heisenberg, thought similarly about creativity and discovery in science:

> A great scientific discovery . . . is often described as an inspiration or a special gift of grace which comes to the researcher when and as it pleases, like the answer from "another authority" and then almost without effort on his part. It is never viewed as the inevitable result of his research effort. Here we find the often disturbing and happy experience: "It is not I; I have not done this." Still, in a certain way it is I—yet not the ego . . . but . . . a more comprehensive self.[131]

Jung conceived of a timeless reservoir of information not unlike Edison's image of "impressions from the Universe at large":

> As a matter of fact we have actually known everything all along; for all these things are always there, only we are not there for them. The possibility of the deepest insight existed at all times, but we were always too far away from it. . . . Originally we were all born out of a world of wholeness and in the first years of life are still completely contained

in it. There we have all knowledge without knowing it. Later we lose it, and call it progress when we
remember it again.[132]

The unfolding of this knowledge is revelatory. It cannot be
manipulated. As Aldous Huxley said,

> Understanding is not inherited, nor can it be labo-
> riously acquired. It is something which, when cir-
> cumstances are favorable, comes to us, so to say,
> of its own accord. All of us are knowers, all the
> time; it is only occasionally and in spite of our-
> selves that we directly understand the mystery of
> given reality.[133]

Still, we are not helpless. Although knowledge cannot be
commanded, it can be invited. We can set the stage for revelation. This seeming paradox has been emphasized repeatedly in
the world's great spiritual traditions. Speaking from the Chris-
tian tradition, Huston Smith says, "Everything is a gift, but
nothing is free."[134] Vivekananda, from the Hindu perspective,
agrees: "The wind of God's grace is always blowing, but you
must raise your sail," while the message from Islam is the same.
As the Sufi mystic Bastami said, "The knowledge of God cannot be attained by seeking, but only those who seek it find it."[135]

Resistance

It may seem disrespectful to suggest that prejudice, intolerance, and bias influence attitudes of scientists toward the nature of consciousness and the way the mind works, because scientists are supposed to weigh facts objectively. But every scientist knows there is a shadow side to the profession, in which narrow-mindedness has always existed.

Open minds toward the evidence we have examined can be hard to come by. Closed minds, of course, are nothing new—not just toward consciousness-related phenomena, but toward new developments in the physical sciences as well.[136] During the early twentieth century, plate tectonics and continental drift were hotly debated in the field of geophysics. The eminent geophysicist Sir Edward Bullard commented on this debate in words that apply to the current arguments about consciousness-related phenomena:

> There is always a strong inclination for a body of professionals to oppose an unorthodox view. Such a group has a considerable investment in orthodoxy: they have learned to interpret a large body of data in terms of the old view, and they have prepared lectures and perhaps written books with the old background. To think the whole subject through again when one is no longer young is not easy and involves admitting a partially misspent youth. . . . Clearly it is more prudent to keep quiet,

to be a moderate defender of orthodoxy, or to maintain that all is doubtful, sit on the fence, and wait in
statesmanlike ambiguity for more data. . . .[137]

Max Planck, the founder of quantum mechanics, con-
fronted this problem. He famously said, "A new scientific truth
does not triumph by convincing its opponents and making
them see the light, but rather because its opponents eventually
die, and a new generation grows up that is familiar with it."[138]
Or as Planck's view is often paraphrased, "Science changes
funeral by funeral."

Planck's observation is especially applicable to medicine, my
field. I have many excellent colleagues who recoil from any view
that contradicts physicalism. This is not surprising. We physicians are continually assured, from premed days forward, that
physicalism is valid. For instance, in a cameo of the materialistic
outlook, the outstanding neuroscientist Antonio Damasio, of the
University of Southern California, confidently predicted in 1999,
the final year of "The Decade of the Brain," which was designated
by United States President George H. W. Bush:

In an effort that continues to gain momentum,
virtually all the functions studied in traditional
psychology—perception, learning, and memory—
are being understood in terms of their brain
underpinnings. The mystery behind many of these
functions are being solved, one by one, and it is

now apparent that even consciousness, the towering problem in the field, is likely to be elucidated
before too long.[139]

Similarly, philosopher Stan V. McDaniel of Sonoma State
University declared that "the mind, self, and consciousness are
now entirely within the purview of neuroscience. It follows that
all other theories of the mind . . . are consigned to the trash
heap."[140]

The trash heap is actually a mild sentence for dissenting
views; burning is sometimes recommended by dedicated physicalists. When Cambridge biologist Rupert Sheldrake hypothe-
sized that the form and function of living and nonliving entities
are influenced by nonmaterial fields, and provided extensive
evidence for such in his 1981 book *A New Science of Life*, Sir
John Maddox, the editor of *Nature*, condemned it as "a book
for burning."[141] It was a punishment that Galileo, who feared
burning, and Giordano Bruno, who experienced it, would have
understood.

CONSCIOUSNESS AS FUNDAMENTAL

The centrality of consciousness in the elaboration of what we
call reality is not a radical idea, but one that has a long and sto-
ried history since humans began to record such things. This
view did not cease to exist with the advent of modern science;
its proponents have simply been ignored. Examples include
Erwin Schrödinger:

Although I think that life may be the result of an accident, I do not think that of consciousness. Consciousness cannot be accounted for in physical terms. For consciousness is absolutely fundamental. It cannot be accounted for in terms of anything else.[142]

Max Planck, the founder of quantum mechanics, said:

I regard consciousness as fundamental. I regard matter as derivative from consciousness. We cannot get behind consciousness. Everything that we talk about, everything that we regard as existing, postulates consciousness.[143]

Near the end of his life, Planck further stated,

As a man who has devoted his whole life to the most clear headed science, to the study of matter, I can tell you as a result of my research about atoms this much: There is no matter as such. All matter originates and exists only by virtue of a force which brings the particle of an atom to vibration and holds this most minute solar system of the atom together. We must assume behind this force the existence of a conscious and intelligent mind. This mind is the matrix of all matter.[144]

Psychiatrist Carl G. Jung said,

> It is almost an absurd prejudice to suppose that existence can only be physical. As a matter of fact, the only form of existence of which we have immediate knowledge is psychic. We might as well say, on the contrary, that physical existence is a mere inference, since we know of matter only in so far as we perceive psychic images mediated by the senses.[145]

From the foregoing, it may seem as if the defenders of a beyond-the-brain view of consciousness are mainly physicists, consciousness researchers, and philosophers, but I am pleased to report that many of my fellow physicians are also waking up to an expanded view of the nature of consciousness, such as neurosurgeon Wilder Penfield. I could cite many additional examples, but one shall suffice—the late physician Lewis Thomas, former dean of New York University Medical School and Yale School of Medicine and, later, director of research and president of the Sloan Kettering Institute in New York, now Memorial Sloan Kettering Cancer Center. Thomas was a no-nonsense physician and bioscientist. He also was a gifted poet and graceful essayist. Among the things he questioned was the destiny of consciousness following bodily death. In his National Book Award–winning book of essays, *The Lives of a Cell* (1974), he wrote:

> There is still that permanent vanishing of con-
> sciousness to be accounted for. Are we to be stuck
> forever with this problem? Where on Earth does
> it go? Is it simply stopped dead in its tracks, lost
> in humans, wasted? Considering the tendency
> of nature to find uses for complex and intricate
> mechanisms, this seems to me unnatural. I prefer
> to think of it somehow as separated off at the fil-
> aments of its attachment, and drawn like an easy
> breath back into the membrane of its origin, a fresh
> memory for a biophysical nervous system....[146]

As part of this "biophysical nervous system," Thomas suggested that our separate brains might be undergoing a kind of
functional "fusion," uniting separate minds in a greater whole
that resembles a collective view of consciousness or Mind at
Large:

> We pass thoughts around, from mind to mind, so
> compulsivel y and with such speed that the brains
> of mankind often appear, functionally, to be under-
> going fusion. . . . Maybe the thoughts we gener-
> ate today and flick around from mind to mind . . .
> are the primitive precursors of more complicated,
> polymerized structures that will come later....[147]

THE STUFFING IN THE KEYHOLE

What a piece of work is a man! How noble in reason,
how infinite in faculty! In form and moving how express
and admirable! In action how like an Angel! in appre-
hension how like a god!

　　—WILLIAM SHAKESPEARE, *Hamlet,* ACT 2, SCENE 2

Novelist Arthur Koestler wrote, "[We are] Peeping Toms at the keyhole of eternity. But at least we can try to take the stuffing out of the keyhole, which blocks even our limited view."[148]

The view of conscious we have explored requires removing the stuffing from the keyhole. If we manage to do so, we shall likely experience Havel's "something higher"—a clearer glimpse of our consciousness, Mind at Large, the Universal or One Mind, the Absolute—not a complete view, for that is beyond our capacity, but a resplendent vision that is as intrinsic to our humanity as our breath and heartbeat. This magnificent view is CPR for the far side of human experience, a vigorous resuscitation of the fact that our consciousness is far more than we have recently taken it to be: that it is eternal, infinite, and one.

Consciousness Is Mind Beyond Space and Time: The New Paradigm

by Ervin Laszlo

"WHAT IS CONSCIOUSNESS?" IS NOT A RHETORI-
CAL QUESTION. We experience consciousness
throughout our life; it is the most direct and
intimate aspect of our existence. We think that we know what
it is. But this is not necessarily the case. As Jean Houston and
Larry Dossey observe, consciousness is not what we, and most
people in today's world, think it is.

Modern commonsense realism, supported by the mainstream philosophy known as classical empiricism, claims that
"there is nothing in the mind that was not first in the eye"[1]—
meaning that everything that enters into our consciousness
comes through the nerve impulses transmitted by our senses.
Our consciousness is a stream of sensations—images, sounds,
tastes, odors and textures—and all elements of this stream
originate in sensory perceptions. Abstract thought is but a
combination of the elements of this stream, and feelings, values, and other "subjective" elements are what we ourselves add
to the stream: they are not part of the world around us. The
world is given to us through our bodily senses. This is the old,
and today still dominant paradigm.

The old paradigm rests on a mistaken argument. We know that our brain coordinates the processes that take place in our body, so it must be that it also coordinates the processes that convey information from our senses. The answer to the question "what is consciousness?" must be that it is a product of the workings of the brain. This answer is woefully inadequate. Consciousness is more, far more, than a product of the brain.

This is a bold claim. Let us look at the evidence.

It turns out that there are dimensions of consciousness that are beyond the reach of the brain and the bodily senses. We can enter a state of mind where such "beyond-the-brain" experiences open for us, time and again. Artists, poets, creative people and "psychic" individuals have this enlarged dimension of consciousness. It is a regular feature of their experience.

In today's world, the wider and deeper dimensions of consciousness are neglected and ignored. Modern people are convinced that consciousness beyond the brain is just fantasy. And because they are convinced that there cannot be consciousness beyond the brain, they do not experience consciousness beyond their brain. After all, we not only believe what we experience, we also experience what we believe—and only, or mostly, what we believe. If we are sure that something is not real and so cannot be experienced, we are not likely to experience it.

THERE IS CONSCIOUSNESS BEYOND THE SENSES

There are elements of human consciousness that transcend the body and the brain. They are not just fantasy. Telepathy, for

example, has been extensively studied. Telepathic communication—communication beyond the reach of the eye and ear—
has been found to exist among people who are closely knit,
whether through kinship (it is frequent among identical twins)
or through emotional bonds between friends, spouses, or lov-
ers. Anthropologists also find that certain indigenous peoples
regularly communicate beyond the range of their senses.

Another extrasensory dimension of consciousness is known
as remote viewing. Ever since Russell Targ and Harold E. Puthoff
published their groundbreaking experiments in the 1970s,[2] the
remote-viewing phenomenon has been studied experimentally.
It turns out that it occurs in a significant segment of the people
who seriously attempt it. It surfaces in the form of an intuition
of forms or images that correspond to sights or things that are
too remote to be seen, yet can be grasped in an intuitive, but
veridical way.

Dramatic and traumatic events often trigger yet another
form of perception beyond the range of the senses. These make
up the out-of-body experience (OBE). In this experience, the
subject sees the world from a perspective beyond his or her eyes.
The most common perspective is a point just below the ceil-
ing, although it can also be above the rooftop or even higher. In
a recent survey of a cross-section of the American population,
ten percent of participants said that they have found themselves
"outside of their body" at least once in their life.

In an OBE, it is not eyesight that produces the perception:
the visual experience is fundamentally different from normal

sight. It occurs even in blind people.[3] In Kenneth Ring's experiments on OBEs of the blind, more than eighty percent of congenitally blind individuals described their surroundings in their OBE in vivid detail. Their visual experience often included a 360-degree vision of high acuity. According to Ring, it is not the subjects' eyes that start to see; rather, "the mind itself sees; but more in the sense of 'understanding' or 'taking in' than of visual perception as such."[4] This is even more astonishing than the claim that the eyes begin to see. It indicates that there are forms of perception that transcend the range of the bodily senses.

Then there is the experience of people who claim to be psychic. Psychic mediums, often in a state of trance, "channel" experiences that did not reach them through sensory means. Channeling can occur through clairvoyance (seeing apparitions), clairaudience (hearing voices), or clairsentience (physical sensations), or a combination of the three. Skeptics dismiss these experiences as inventions of the mediums. There are, however, documented cases of mediums coming up with information they could not have created themselves. A case in point is the game of chess between a live grandmaster and a grandmaster who has been dead for decades, which I discussed in a previous book and summarize here.[5]

Wolfgang Eisenbeiss, an amateur chess-player, engaged the trance-medium Robert Rollans to transmit the moves of a game to be played with Viktor Korchnoi, the world's third-ranking grandmaster. Rollans was also tasked to find an opponent from a list of deceased grandmasters, whom he would contact by extraordinary means, in a trance state. On June 15, 1985, Geza Maroczy (1870–1951), the world's third-ranking grandmaster in the year 1900, responded and accepted the challenge.

Korchnoi and Maroczy began a game that was frequently interrupted due to Korchnoi's poor health and frequent travels. It lasted seven years and eight months. Speaking through Rollans, Maroczy gave his moves in the standard form: for example, "5. A3 – Bxc3+". Korchnoi gave his own moves to Rollans in the same form, but by sensory ordinary communication. Every move was analyzed and recorded. The game was played at the grandmaster level and exhibited the precise style for which Maroczy had been known. It ended on February 11, 1993, when Maroczy resigned at the forty-eighth move. Subsequent analysis showed that it was a wise decision: Korchnoi would have checkmated him five moves later.

In this case, the medium Rollans channeled information that he did not possess in his ordinary state of consciousness. Moreover, this information was so precise that it is unlikely that anyone else near to or, assuming some form of telepathy among the living, even far from, Rollans would have possessed it. The source of this information is anomalous—a puzzle, at least, for the prevalent paradigm of consciousness.

THERE IS CONSCIOUSNESS BEYOND THE BRAIN

Another anomalous feature of consciousness is that which appears when the brain of the individual is not functioning, and even when it is clinically dead. This condition is implied by psychic mediums who channel the consciousness of people who are already dead. But it is even more strikingly and convincingly the case in regard to people who recount their own experiences while they were brain-dead. These are the so-called near-death experiences: (NDEs).

Research on NDEs is widespread. Clinical studies show that sometimes there is conscious experience when the electroencephalograph (EEG) wave becomes a flat line. When that happens, the brain is believed to be inoperative. If it does not return to a normal state within a matter of minutes, the organism enters irreversible coma and dies.

A brief EEG flatline period is not exceptional and can be survived. When the heart stops beating (which is often the case during a massive heart attack), the brain flatlines in about fifteen seconds. It takes about a minute, however, for resuscitation equipment to come online, even in a modern ambulance or hospital, which means that many patients remain without a functioning brain for nearly a minute. Currently, physicians consider a patient lost if he or she suffers two twenty-minute EEG flatlines within four hours. Even that span of time is unduly pessimistic, however, as in some cases people recover after more than twenty minutes without a heartbeat and hence without a functioning brain.

While the brain is flatlining, consciousness is assumed to have ceased. But this is not always the case. The literature on the NDE is full of documented cases of conscious experience during a flatline. One of the most remarkable is that of Pamela

Reynolds.[6] The following was her experience while under full anesthesia during major surgery.

> I heard a mechanical noise and it reminded me of a dentist's drill. Then, I just sort of popped out of the top of my head. In this state, I was able to see the situation very clearly. I remember that my doctor had an instrument in his hand that looked like the handle of my electric toothbrush. It had a dent in it—a groove at the top where the tip appeared to go into the handle, but when I saw it, there was no tip. I looked down and saw a box; it reminded me of my father's box of tools when I was a child. That's where he kept his pocket wrenches. At about the same moment that I saw the instrument, I heard a woman's voice. I believe it was the voice of my cardiologist. She was saying that my veins and arteries were too small to extract blood from them and the surgeon told her to try the other side.

Reynolds then reported some frequent but unverifiable experiences, such as seeing long-dead relatives. Her perceptions on the operating table, however, were verified. The team of doctors performing the operation confirmed that what she reported is what she would have seen, had her brain been functioning normally. But her brain was not only anaesthetized by standard procedures, it was subjected to the special treatment known as standstill. This involves diverting all blood flow from the brain to a circulatory system outside the body and is used only when the patient would die without immediate intervention. Reynolds had a large vascular tumor at the base of the brain that could have burst at any time, so her physician decided to undertake the high-risk standstill procedure. The operating table was strongly tilted to ensure that her brain would not contain a single drop of blood, and her body temperature was lowered to 59.9 degrees Fahrenheit to prevent the formation of the irreversible brain lesions that come in less than five minutes after cessation of blood flow to the brain. Reynolds' EEG quickly flatlined and stayed flat for nearly an hour. During that time she had the conscious experiences she subsequently recounted.

The experiences she recounted, and her physicians confirmed, are surprising, but far from exceptional. There are now an estimated six million cases of NDE—conscious experience in the absence of a functioning brain. The core features of the experience have been collected and codified by serious investigators, such as Pim van Lommel, Raymond Moody, Bruce Greyson, and Anthony Peake among others. These include hearing loud noises early in the process; moving through a long, dark tunnel; seeing a white or gold light that is separate from oneself; seeing religious figures such as Jesus, Buddha or Moses; having a panoramic review of one's life and learning its merits and demerits; and indications that the experience is meant to edify those who undergo it.

THERE IS CONSCIOUSNESS BEYOND LIFE

The NDE shows that consciousness does not always cease when the brain becomes temporarily inoperative. There are dimensions of consciousness still more surprising than this. They suggest that consciousness does not cease even when the experiencing individual has died.

Evidence for this remarkable "survival" dimension of consciousness is provided by the reports of psychic mediums who channel persons who identify themselves as dead, yet in some way are still living. This was what the deceased chess grandmaster previously discussed appears to have done. In response to the medium Robert Rollans' search for a chess partner, Geza Marozcy, speaking through Rollans, said:

> I will be at your disposal in this peculiar game of chess for two reasons. First, because I also want to do something to aid mankind living on Earth to become convinced that death does not end everything, but instead the mind is separated from the physical body and comes up to us in a new world, where individual life continues to manifest itself in a new unknown dimension. Second, being a Hungarian patriot, I want to guide the eyes of the world into the direction of my beloved Hungary. . . .[7]

There are numerous cases of a channeled consciousness identifying itself as the consciousness of a deceased person.

One of the most remarkable cases is the message channeled by Rosemary Brown from the late philosopher Bertrand Russell. Lord Russell was an agnostic. He always claimed skepticism about the probability, if not the mere possibility, of life after death. After he died, however, he came up with a detailed account of his own postmortem experience.

> After breathing my last breath in my mortal body, I found myself in some sort of extension of existence that held no parallel, as far as I could estimate, in the material dimension I had recently experienced. . . . Now, here I was, still the same I, with capacities to think and observe sharpened to an incredible degree. I felt earth-life suddenly very unreal almost as though it had never happened. It took me quite a long time to understand this feeling until I realized at last that matter is certainly illusory although it does exist in actuality; the material world seemed now nothing more than a seething, changing restless sea of indeterminate density and volume.[8]

In the message channeled by Brown, Russell took pains to affirm that he, Bertrand Russell, was the one who sent the message. He was in possession of a functioning consciousness, even if not of a living body.

You may not believe that it is I, Bertrand Arthur William Russell, who am saying these things, and perhaps there is no conclusive proof that I can offer through this somewhat restricted medium. Those with an ear to hear may catch the echo of my voice in my phrases, the tenor of my tongue in my tautology; those who do not wish to hear will no doubt conjure up a whole table of tricks to disprove my retrospective rhetoric.

Russell was not the only example. F. W. H. Myers (1843–1901), a classical scholar in England, developed a great interest in psychic phenomena; he was a founding member of the Society for Psychical Research and became its president in 1900. He was not a skeptic, but like Russell, he was aware of the need to lend credibility to his messages. His method of "cross-correspondences" proved to be remarkably effective in achieving this. Myers' method is to send messages that are meaningless by themselves, but acquire significance when joined together. Several mediums receive elements of the message, and the fragments go beyond the knowledge and information available to the individual mediums. They do not know each other and do not know they are receiving complementary messages. It is highly improbable that they would invent the messages themselves, since even joined together, deciphering them requires specialized knowledge (in Myers' case, advanced knowledge of classical English literature).

In 1903, two years after Myers' death, *Human Personality and its Survival of Bodily Death*, a two-volume work of 1,360 pages, was compiled and published. It was dictated by Myers to the trance medium Geraldine Cummins, who had never met Myers; she was a small girl when Myers died. It describes his experiences in the discarnate realm, giving details of the various planes of existence his consciousness encountered after the demise of his body.

Contrary to popular belief, it appears that contact and communication with the consciousness of a deceased individual does not require exceptional gifts or capacities. Apparitions, visions, and deathbed visitations have been reported throughout history, and discarnate beings were said to appear suddenly and communicate with ordinary people. The first systematic study of these phenomena was undertaken in 1882 by the Society for Psychical Research in England, and this pioneering effort was followed by similar research in the United States. In 1925, the French astronomer Camille Flammarion published a milestone study, *Death and its Mystery,* in which he described scores of cases of spontaneous contact with deceased individuals. In May 1988, Bill and Judy Guggenheim undertook an in-depth study of what they called ADC: After-Death Communication. They collected more than 3,300 first-hand accounts from people who were convinced that they were contacted by recently deceased family members. Their book *Hello from Heaven*[9] contains 353 of the most robust of these accounts.

ADC appears to be available to nearly all people. It usually comes about spontaneously, but it can also be intentionally induced. Once the required receptive state of consciousness is attained, people communicate on their own. Psychotherapist Allan Botkin, head of the Center for Grief and Traumatic Loss in Libertyville, Illinois, claims that he and his colleagues have successfully induced after-death communication in more than three thousand patients. Communication can be established even with now-deceased people whom the subject had never met in life. Combat veterans, for example, experience communication with the anonymous enemy soldier they killed and for whom they grieve.

Added to spontaneous or induced first-hand experiences are messages transmitted by manmade instruments such as radios, television sets, tape recorders, and telephones. These cases are also widespread and they are extensively investigated. While there is no definitive agreement as to how the anomalous voices—and in some cases images—come about, most investigators maintain that they do come about. They are cases of instrumental transcommunication (ITC). Although in some cases a living psychic seems necessary for the messages to appear, they often come through also in their absence.

The thousands of documented cases of NDE, OBE, ADC and ITC provide meaningful evidence that there are dimensions of consciousness that transcend the range of the bodily senses. Psychiatrist Stanislav Grof collected such experiences over several decades and categorized them in what he calls a "cartography of transpersonal experiences." The experiences fall into three categories. The first category "involves primarily transcendence of the usual spatial barriers, or the limitations of the 'skin-encapsulated ego,' as Alan Watts referred to it." Grof specifies:

> Here belong experiences of merging with another person into a state that can be called "dual unity," assuming the identity of another person, identifying with the consciousness of an entire group of people (e.g., all mothers of the world, the entire population of India, or all the inmates of concentration camps), or even experiencing an extension of consciousness that seems to encompass all of humanity. Experiences of this kind have been repeatedly described in the spiritual literature of the world.

> One can even transcend the limits of human experience and identify with the consciousness of various animals, plants, or even with a form of consciousness that seems to be associated with inorganic objects and processes. In the extremes, it is possible to experience consciousness of the entire biosphere, of our planet, or the entire material universe. Incredible and absurd as it might seem to a Westerner committed to materialistic philosophy

and to the Cartesian-Newtonian paradigm, these experiences suggest that everything that we can experience in our everyday state of consciousness as an object has in the holotropic [nonordinary] states of consciousness a corresponding subjective representation. It is as if everything in the universe has its objective and subjective aspect, the way it is described in the great spiritual philosophies of the East. For example, in Hinduism all that exists is seen as a manifestation of Brahman and in Taoism as a transformation of the Tao.

The second category, according to Grof,

. . . is characterized primarily by overcoming of temporal rather than spatial boundaries, by transcendence of linear time. . . . The vivid reliving of important memories from infancy and of the trauma of birth . . . can continue farther and involve authentic fetal and embryonal memories from different periods of intrauterine life. It is not even unusual to experience, on the level of cellular consciousness, full identification with the sperm and the ovum at the time of conception. But the historical regression does not stop even here; it is possible to have experiences from the lives of one's human or animal ancestors, and those that seem

to be coming from the racial and collective unconscious as described by C. G. Jung. Quite frequently,
the experiences that seem to be happening in other
cultures and historical periods are associated with
a sense of personal remembering (*déjà vu* or *déjà
vécu*); people then talk about reliving of memories
from past lives, from previous incarnations.

The third category is "even stranger" in Grof's estimation.
It is where

> ... consciousness seems to extend into realms and
> dimensions that the Western industrial culture
> does not even consider to be "real." Here belong
> numerous encounters or even identification with
> deities and demons of various cultures and other
> archetypal figures, visits to mythological land-
> scapes, and communication with discarnate
> beings, spirit guides, superhuman entities, extra-
> terrestrials, and inhabitants of parallel universes.
> Additional examples in this category are visions
> and intuitive understanding of universal symbols,
> such as the cross, the Nile cross or ankh, the swas-
> tika, the pentacle, the six-pointed star, or the yin
> yang sign.[10]

Modern people dismiss transpersonal experiences as mere imagination. But the problem with such dismissal is that some of them convey veridical information about the world. This is true especially of the first and second category. These include not only contact with things and events that are spatially or temporally distant from the experiencer, but also actual communication with an entity that appears to be a discarnate consciousness.

An unbiased assessment of the evidence I have just reviewed, together with that presented in this book by Jean Houston and Larry Dossey, calls for a revision of the dominant paradigm of consciousness. The range of human consciousness is too wide to have been produced by the brain. The question then arises: if the current paradigm rests on faulty assumptions (since consciousness is not a product of the brain), then what is the correct paradigm? What is the real nature of consciousness?

Consciousness is the Manifestation of Mind Beyond Space and Time: The New Paradigm?

Evidently, the fact that consciousness transcends the brain is not an indication that consciousness would be independent of the brain. The brain has an obvious role in eliciting the stream of sensations that makes up consciousness. But it does not follow that the brain would actually produce that stream.

It is far from clear how a set of neurons could transform electrical and biochemical information into qualitative experience. Nobel laureate neurophysiologist Roger Sperry noted that

the "centermost processes of the brain with which consciousness is presumably associated are simply not understood."[11]
Another Nobel laureate, physicist Eugene P. Wigner, noted that
"we have at present not the vaguest idea how to connect the
physico-chemical processes with the state of mind."[12]

There are elements of the stream of our sensations that are
still more problematic, they surpass the bounds of the information available to the senses. These elements, some of which
have been enumerated by Stanislav Grof in his cartography of
transcendental experiences, could not have been conveyed to
the brain by the bodily senses. They could have been captured,
however, by subneuronal networks in the brain and transmitted as elements of consciousness.[13]

In light of the new-paradigm transmission theory, elements of consciousness exist also beyond the brain, in the same
way that a program broadcast over the air exists beyond the
TV set that receives it. The signals of the transmission exist
even when they are not captured by a receiver, although in that
case there are no perceptible images and sounds. Likewise, consciousness exists in the world even when the brain is "turned
off" and phenomena of consciousness are not displayed.

That the brain transmits rather than produces consciousness is an age-old intuition. It was revived by William James
in his 1899 "Ingersoll Lecture on Immortality."[14]James spoke
of a "veiled" domain from which information would be transmitted by the brain. The transmission theory, he pointed out,

can account for phenomena that are anomalous for the production theory: if the brain only transmits and does not produce consciousness, consciousness need not cease when the brain is inoperative. Conscious experience beyond the brain is no longer esoteric: it is possible and comprehensible.

Consciousness is a Hologram Beyond Space and Time

The new paradigm holds that consciousness is a natural phenomenon in the natural world: it does not depend on the brain for its existence. If so, we must say what consciousness actually is. On the basis of recent developments at the cutting edge of science, we can say with some assurance that it is a hologram— more exactly, the nonlocal projection of a cosmic hologram.

What is a hologram? A hologram is the product of the interference of two sets of waves: a set of object waves and a set of reference waves. The object waves are directed towards the object. They encode the intensity changes and phase shifts reflecting the features of the object as the waves reach it and are emitted away from it. When the reference waves are directed back toward the re-modulated object waves, they create an interference pattern that records the phase-shifts of the object waves relative to the reference waves. This pattern encodes the phase-shift information from which, through a Fourier (more exactly, a Gabor) transform, a static, three-dimensional image of the object is then constituted.

The theory that the consciousness we experience is a hologram, or rather, the projection of a hologram, rests on the
widely discussed holographic theory of the universe. According
to this theory, the three-dimensional (3D) things and events
we observe in the world are holographic projections of two-dimensional (2D) codes at the periphery of space-time, or possibly in another universe. If we accept the current view of the
dimensionality of space-time, then the space-time of our world
is four-dimensional, if not ten or eleven-dimensional. In that
case, however, the codes of which things in the universe are
projections cannot be at the periphery of space-time, for that
periphery is two-dimensional. The codes must be in a field
or medium the traditional wisdom schools called the fifth or
higher dimension, David Bohm named the implicate order, and
I call the Akashic Field or Deep Dimension. Regardless of how
we name it, it is clear that it is not an order *within* space-time,
but *beyond* it.

The holographic universe theory was put forward by David
Bohm in an influential book in 1980, and the informational
aspects of the theory have been worked out by astrophysicist
Jacob Bekenstein in 2003.[15] Empirical support for the theory
surfaced in 2013 when Fermilab physicist Craig Hogan pro-
posed a hypothesis that could be tested against observation.
He suggested that the fluctuations observed by the German
gravity-wave detector GEO600 may be due to the graininess of
space (according to string theory, at super-small scale, space is
not smooth but patterned by minuscule ripples, or "grainy").

It turned out that the inhomogeneities found by GEO600 are not gravity waves. However, they could be ripples in the fine structure of space. This would be the case if they were 3D projections of the 2D Planck-dimensional codes that paper the periphery—the surface—of space-time. If the grains found by GEO600 would be the precisely the size that would be produced by 2D Planck-dimensional codes at the space-time periphery, Hogan's hypothesis would be confirmed. Subsequent observations confirmed that they are.

Further support for the holographic universe theory came in the work of Yoshifumi Hyakutake and colleagues at Ibaraki University in Japan. They computed the internal energy of a black hole, the position of its event horizon, its entropy and several other properties based on the predictions of string theory and the effects of virtual particles. They concluded that the internal energy of a black hole and the internal energy of the corresponding lower-dimensional cosmos are the same. Black holes, as well as the cosmos as a whole, appear to be holographic.[16]

Then Leonard Susskind and Gerard 't Hooft suggested that if a 3D star can be encoded on a black hole's 2D event horizon, the same may be true of the whole of the universe. The universe's space-time boundary is 42 billion light years from us: it is the periphery of the territory covered by light since the Big Bang.

This 42-billion light-year boundary could code three dimensional objects in space-time, but not, however, higher-dimensional objects. If objects were more than three-dimensional their codes must be more than two-dimensional. We must then look to the above-mentioned field, medium or dimension as the original ground of phenomena in the universe.

The holographic theory is the currently most plausible account of the nature of space-time and of the objects and events that populate it. It is not necessarily limited to physical phenomena. The consciousness that appears in space-time could also be the projection of beyond-spacetime holographic codes. We could regard these codes as manifestations of mind in the cosmos beyond space and beyond time.

The new-paradigm holographic theory of consciousness offers a science-based, minimally speculative explanation of a vast range of otherwise puzzling phenomena—phenomena that vastly exceed the range of human sensory experience.

The beyond-space-time hologram is an enduring element in nature. It connects consciousness phenomena across space as well as time. It is the cosmic mind that conserves and conveys information on the past as well as on the present, and interconnects phenomena throughout space. Thus we can understand why communication between individual consciousnesses turns out to be nonlocal: not limited by the speed or range of information-transmission in space and time.

The nonlocality of consciousness is widely recognized. Astronaut-turned-consciousness researcher Edgar Mitchell noted:

It is likely that most, if not all, subtle, ephemeral and unexplained phenomena associated with subjective experience are connected, directly or indirectly, with the phenomenon of nonlocality. . . . Nonlocality and the nonlocal quantum hologram provide the only testable mechanism discovered to date which offers a possible solution to the host of enigmatic observations and data associated with consciousness and such consciousness phenomena.[17]

It is time to state our conclusions. Einstein said that in science we seek the scheme of thought that can tie together the observed facts. The new paradigm ties together the known facts of consciousness, as well as the facts that are beyond the ken of the old-paradigm theories. It is more embracing and consistent than the brain-production theory. It may be the best answer we can give today to the perennial question, *what is consciousness?*[18]

LIVING THE ANSWER: A PERSONAL CREDO

My consciousness—the same as the consciousness of all living beings—is the localized yet nonlocal manifestation of mind beyond space and time. As a conscious human being, I am an intrinsic and infinite part of this mind. My personal consciousness is a localized but nonlocal manifestation of it.

My "re-cognition" of this ancient insight changes my understanding of who I am, and changes the way I think of myself, of others, and of the world. The sixteen points below summarize my new understanding, and the kind of values, beliefs and attitudes it inspires in me, a being who realizes that his or her consciousness is an intrinsic part of the world.[19]

1. I am part of the world. The world is not outside of me, and I am not outside of the world. The world is in me, and I am in the world.

2. I am part of nature, and nature is part of me. I am what I am in my communication and communion with all living things. I am an irreducible and coherent whole with the web of life on the planet.

3. I am part of society, and society is part of me. I am what I am in my communication and communion with my fellow humans. I am an irreducible and coherent whole with the community of humans on the planet.

4. I am more than a skin-and-bone material organism: my body and its cells and organs are manifestations of what is truly me: a self-sustaining, self-evolving dynamic system arising, persisting,

and evolving in interaction with everything
around me.

5. I am one of the highest, most evolved manifestations of the drive toward coherence and wholeness
in the universe. All systems drive toward coherence and wholeness in interaction with all other
systems, and my essence is this cosmic drive. It is
the same essence, the same spirit that is inherent
in all the things that arise and evolve in nature,
whether on this planet or elsewhere in the infinite
reaches of space and time.

6. There are no absolute boundaries and divisions in
this world, only transition points where one set of
relations yields prevalence to another. In me, in
this self-maintaining and self-evolving coherence-
and wholeness-oriented system, the relations that
integrate the cells and organs of my body are prevalent. Beyond my body other relations gain prevalence: those that drive toward coherence and
wholeness in society and in nature.

7. The separate identity I attach to other humans and
other things is but a convenient convention that
facilitates my interaction with them. My family

and my community are just as much "me" as the organs of my body. My body and mind, my family and my community, are interacting and interpenetrating, variously prevalent elements in the network of relations that encompasses all things in nature and the human world.

8. The whole gamut of concepts and ideas that separates my identity, or the identity of any person or community, from the identity of other persons and communities are manifestations of this convenient but arbitrary convention. There are only gradients distinguishing individuals from each other and from their environment and no real divisions or boundaries. There are no "others" in the world: we are all living systems and we are all part of each other.

9. Attempting to maintain the system I know as "me" through ruthless competition with the system I know as "you" is a grave mistake: it could damage the integrity of the embracing whole that frames both your life and mine. I cannot preserve my own life and wholeness by damaging that whole, even if damaging a part of it seems to bring me short-term advantage. When I harm you, or anyone else around me, I harm myself.

10. Collaboration, not competition, is the royal road to the wholeness that hallmarks healthy systems in the world. Collaboration calls for empathy and solidarity, and ultimately for love. I do not and cannot love myself if I do not love you and others around me: we are part of the same whole and so are part of each other.

11. The idea of "self-defense," or even of "national defense," needs to be rethought. Patriotism, if it aims to eliminate adversaries by force, and heroism, even in the well-meaning execution of that aim, are mistaken aspirations. A patriot and a hero who brandishes a sword or a gun is an enemy also to himself. Every weapon intended to hurt or kill is a danger to all. Comprehension, conciliation, and forgiveness are not signs of weakness; they are signs of courage.

12. The "good" for me and for every person in the world is not the possession and accumulation of personal wealth. Wealth, in money or in any material resource, is but a means for maintaining myself in my environment. As exclusively mine, it commandeers part of the resources that all things need to share if they are to live and to thrive. Exclusive wealth is a threat to all people in

the human community. And because I am a part of this community, in the final count it is a threat also to me, and to all who hold it.

13. Beyond the sacred whole we recognize as the world in its totality, only life and its development have what philosophers call intrinsic value; all other things have merely instrumental value: value insofar as they add to or enhance intrinsic value. Material things in the world, and the energies and substances they harbor or generate, have value only if and insofar they contribute to life and wellbeing in the web of life on this earth.

14. Every healthy person has pleasure in giving: it is a higher pleasure than having. I am healthy and whole when I value giving over having. The true measure of my accomplishment and excellence is my readiness to give. Not the amount of what I give is the measure of my accomplishment and excellence, but the relation between what I give, and what my family and I need to live and to thrive.

15. A community that values giving over having is a community of healthy people, oriented toward thriving through empathy, solidarity, and love

among its members. Sharing enhances the community of life, while possessing and accumulating creates demarcation, invites competition, and fuels envy. The share-society is the norm for all the communities of life on the planet; the have-society is typical only of modern-day humanity, and it is an aberration.

I have been part of the aberration of human consciousness in recent times, and now wish to become part of the great wave that overcomes the aberration and heals the wounds inflicted by it. This is my right as well as my duty, as a conscious member of a conscious species on a precious and now critically endangered planet.

Notes

FOREWORD

1. *APA Dictionary of Psychology,* 1st ed., Gary R.VandenBos, ed. (Washington, DC: American Psychological Association, 2007), s.v. "consciousness."

2. Daniel Stoljar, "Physicalism," *The Stanford Encyclopedia of Philosophy,* ed. Edward N. Zalta (2009), accessed August 4, 2015, http://plato.stanford.edu/archives/fall2009/entries/physicalism/.

CONSCIOUSNESS IS THE QUANTUM FIELD OF THE COSMOS

1. J.W.N. Sullivan, "Interviews with the Great Scientists VI: Max Planck," *The Observer,* Jan. 25, 1931, 17.

2. Ervin Laszlo with Gyorgyi Szabo, "The Oneness Declaration: Sixteen Hallmarks of the New Consciousness," *Humanity's Team.* Accessed August 17, 2015. http://www.humanitysteam.org/ErvinLaszlo.

3. Larry Dossey, "Consciousness is Eternal, Infinite and One—A Summing Up," Ervin Laszlo, ed., *What is Consciousness? Three Sages Look Behind the Veil* (New York: SelectBooks, 2016): pg tk.

4. Deepak Chopra, "Summoning the Sacred: Awaken the Divine Within" (lecture, Sedona, AZ, May 30, 2014).

5. Ervin Laszlo, ed., "Consciousness Is a Cosmic Hologram: Modern Science Re-Cognizes an Ancient Insight" in *What is Consciousness? Three Sages Look Behind the Veil* (New York: SelectBooks, 2016): pg tk.

6. T.S. Eliot, "Burnt Norton" in *Four Quartets* (New York: Harcourt Houghton Mifflin, 2014), 13.

7. Walt Whitman, "Full of Life Now" in *Leaves of Grass: A Textual Variorum of the Printed Poems, 1860-1867* (New York: NYU Press, 2008), 407.

Consciousness Is Eternal, Infinite, and One—A Summing Up

1. William James. *The Correspondence of William James* Volume 11, ed. John J. McDermott, et al (Charlottesville, VA: University of Virginia Press; 1992–2004): 143–144.

2. Albert Einstein. Albert Einstein Site Online. Accesed June 2, 2015. http://www.alberteinsteinsite.com/quotes/einsteinquotes.html.

3. Albert Einstein. Wikiquote. Accessed June 2, 2015. http://en.wikiquote.org/wiki/Albert_Einstein.

4. K. Ramakrishna Rao, *Cognitive Anomalies, Consciousness and Yoga*, vol. XVI, part 1 of *History of Science, Philosophy and Culture in Indian Civilization*, ed. D. P. Chattopadhyaya,(New Delhi: Centre for Studies in Civilizations / Matrix, 2011): 335.

5. Roger S. Jones, *Physics as Metaphor* (New York: Plume, 1983): 1.

6. Mario Beauregard, et al, "Manifesto for a post-material science," *Explore: The Journal of Science and Healing.* 10:5 (September–October 2014): 272–274. Accessed April 7, 2015. http://www.explorejournal.com/article/S1550-8307(14)00116-5/pdf.

7. André Malraux quoted in David Hirst, "On the spirituality of the 21st century, Malraux revisited" Last modified January 6, 2009. Researchgate.net. Accessed March 25, 2015. http://www.researchgate.net/post/G_On_the_spirituality_of_the_21st_Century_Malraux_revisited

8. Václav Havel quoted in Delia Popescu, *Political Action in Václav Havel's Thought: The Responsibility of Resistance* (Lanham, MD: Lexington/Rowman & Littlefield, 2012): 83.

9. Václav Havel, Speech to Congress, February 21, 1990 in Jackson J. Spielvogel, *Western Civilization, Volume C: Since 1789*, 8th ed, (Boston: Wadsworth, 2012): 953. See also Everything2.com. Accessed March 24, 2012. http://everything2.com/title/Vaclav+Havel%2527s+address+to+the+US+Congress%252C+21+February+1990.

10. Definition of "materialism." Oxford Dictionaries. Accessed August 18, 2015. http://www.oxforddictionaries.com/us/definition/american_english/materialism.

11. David Lindley, "Response to Robert Lanza," *USA Today*, March 9, 2007, accessed March 15, 2015. http://usatoday30.usatoday.com/tech/science/2007-03-09-lanza-response_N.htm.

12. Daniel C. Dennett quoted in Dennis Overbye, "Free Will: Now You Have It, Now You Don't, *The New York Times*, January 2, 2007, accessed August 18, 2015, http://www.nytimes.com/2007/01/02/science/02free.html?pagewanted=all&_r=0.

13. Jacques Monod, *Chance and Necessity: An Essay on the Natural Philosophy of Modern Biology* (New York: Vintage Books, 1972): 21.

14. Daniel C. Dennett, *Consciousness Explained* (Boston: Back Bay Books, 1992): 406.

15. Francis Crick, *The Astonishing Hypothesis* (New York: Simon & Schuster, 1994): 271.

16. Carl Sagan, T*he Dragons of Eden: Speculations on the Evolution of Human Intelligence* (New York: Random House, 1977): 7.

17. Allan Hobson quoted in *The Neurology of Consciousness: Cognitive Neuroscience and Neuropathology*, eds. Steven Laureys and Giulio Tononi (Salt Lake City, UT: Academic Press, 2008): xi.

18. Steven Weinberg, *The First Three Minutes* (New York: Basic, 1993): 154.

19. Bertrand Russsell, *A Free Man's Worship* (Portland, Me: Thomas Bird Mosher, 1923): 6–7.

20. A. S. Eddington, *Science and the Unseen World* (London: Quaker Books, 2007): 9.

21. Mary Midgley, "Thinking matter," *New Scientist* 200: 2689 (January 3, 2009): 16. See: https://www.newscientist.com/letter/mg20126880-300-thinking-matter/

22. Edward F. Kelly, ed., *Beyond Physicalism: Toward Reconciliation of Science and Spirituality* (Lanham, MD: Rowman & Littlefield, 2015): viii.

23. Charles Eisenstein, "A state of belief is a state of being," *Network Review* 113 (Winter 2013): 3–6.

24. J. C. Eccles, *Facing Reality: Philosophical Adventures by a Brain Scientist* (New York: Springer-Verlag, 1970): 115.

25. Joshua Stern quoted in "The future of consciousness studies," unsigned editorial, *Journal of Consciousness Studies* 4:5–6 (1997): 387.

26. Thomas Henry Huxley quoted in Colin McGinn, *The Mysterious Flame* (New York: Basic Books, 1999): 16.

27. Steven Pinker, *How the Mind Works* (New York: W. W. Norton, 1997): 146.

28. Roger Sperry quoted in Denis Brian, *Genius Talk: Conversations with Nobel Scientists and Other Luminaries* (Amsterdam: Kluwer Academic Publishers 1995): 367.

29. Eugene P. Wigner, "Are We Machines?" in *Proceedings of the American Philosophical Society* 113:2 (April 1969). Accessed February 2, 2010. http://www.jstor.org/stable/985959.

30. Freeman Dyson, "How We Know," *The New York Review of Books* 58:4 (March 10, 2011): 8–12.

31. Karl Giberson, "The man who fell to earth: Interview with Roger Penrose," *Science & Spirit* (March/April 2003): 34–41. Accessed 7 April, 2015. http://quantum.webhost.uits.arizona.edu/prod/sites/default/files/The%20Man%20Who%20Fell%20to%20Earth.pdf.

32. Niehls Bohr quoted in Werner Heisenberg, *Physics and Beyond*, A. J. Pomerans, trans., (New York: Harper & Row, 1971): 88–91.

33. Heisenberg, *Physics and Beyond*, 114.

34. Wilder Penfield, *The Mystery of the Mind: A Critical Study of Consciousness and the Human Brain* (Princeton, NJ: Princeton UP, 1975), 79–81.

35. John Maddox, "The unexpected science to come," *Scientific American* 281:6 (1999): 62–7.

36. Erwin Schrödinger quoted in *Quantum Questions: Mystical Writings of the World's Great Physicists*, ed. Ken Wilbur (Boulder, CO: New Science Library, 1984): 81.

37. David Darling, "Supposing something different: Reconciling science and the afterlife," *OMNI* 17:9 (1995), 4.

38. David Darling, *Soul Search: A Scientist Explores the Afterlife* (New York: Villard, 1995): 155–166.

39. Donald D. Hoffman, Edge: The World Question Center. Last revised 2005. Accessed July 19, 2014. .http://edge.org/q2005/q05_4.html#.

See also: "Consciousness and the Mind-Body Problem," Mind & Matter Vol. 6 (1), 2008: 87–121

40. Daniel Dennett quoted in Dick J. Bierman, "On the nature of anomalous phenomena" in *The Physical Nature of Consciousness*, ed. Philip Van Looke (Philadelphia: John Benjamins, 2001), 269–292.

41. A. J. Ayer, "What I saw when I was dead," *Immortality*, ed. Paul Edwards (Amherst, NY: Prometheus, 1997): 269–75. See also A. J. Ayer, "Postscript to a postmortem," *The Spectator*, October 15, 1988, 205–208 and Peter Foges, "An atheist meets the masters of the universe." Roundtable: Opinions and analysis from *Lapham's Quarterly* writers and editors. Last revised March 8, 2010. Accessed November 21, 2012. http://www.laphamsquarterly.org/roundtable/roundtable/an-atheist-meets-the-masters-of-the-universe.php.

42. William James, *The Will to Believe* (Cambridge, MA: Harvard UP, 1979): 19. See also David Ray Griffin, *Parapsychology, Philosophy, and Spirituality: A Postmodern Exploration* (Albany, NY: SUNY Press, 1997): 29.

43. Edwards, ed.: *Immortality*, v.

44. John Eccles and Daniel N. Robinson, *The Wonder of Being Human: Our Brain & Our Mind* (Boston: Shambhala, 1984): 178.

45. C. G. Jung, *Memories, Dreams, Reflections* (New York: Random House, 1965): 325.

46. George Orwell quoted in John Banville, "Good Man, Bad World," *The New York Review of Books* 50:17 (November 6, 2003): 62–65.

47. C. G. Jung, *The Symbolic Life: Collected Works* vol. 13, R.F.C. Hull, trans.): (Princeton, NJ: Princeton UP, 1976): 68.

48. Richard Feynman quoted in John Boslough, "The Enigma of Time," *National Geographic* 177: 3 (March 1990), 109–132.

49. Ludwig Wittgenstein, "*Tractatus Logico-Philosophicus*: Proposition 6.4311." Wikiquote.org. Accessed April 21, 2015. http://en.wikiquote.org/wiki/Ludwig_Wittgenstein.

50. Marilyn Schlitz, *Death Makes Life Possible: Revolutionary Insights on Living, Dying, and the Continuation of Consciousness* (Louisville, CO: Sounds True, 2015).

51. Ernest Becker, *The Denial of Death* (New York: Free Press, 1997): xvii.

52. Edward F. Kelly, *Beyond Physicalism*, viii.

53. Henry P. Stapp, "Attention, Intention, and Will in Quantum Physics." Physics.lbl.gov. Last modified May 14, 1999. Accessed 2 March, 2015. http://www-physics.lbl.gov/~stapp/jcs.txt.

54. Tara MacIsaac, "A physicist's explanation of why the soul may exist," *The Epoch Times*. Last modified June 24, 2014. Accessed March 2, 2015. http://www.theepochtimes.com/n3/757910-a-physicists-explanation-of-why-the-soul-may-exist/.

55. Margaret Wertheim, "The odd couple," *The Sciences* 39:2 (March-April 1999): 38–43.

56. Menas Kafatos and Robert Nadeau, *The Conscious Universe: Parts and Wholes in Physical Reality* (New York: Springer, 2000).

57. Menas C. Kafatos, "The Spookie Mind," *Huffington Post*. Last modified January 11, 2015. Accessed 11 March, 2015. http://www.huffingtonpost.com/menas-c-kafatos/the-spookie-mind_b_6126772.html.

58. "Karl Popper." The Information Philosopher. Accessed March 25, 2015. http://www.informationphilosopher.com/solutions/philosophers/popper/.

59. Sir John Eccles and Daniel N. Robinson, *The Wonder of Being Human: Our Brain & Our Mind* (Boston: Shambhala, 1984): 38.

60. Eccles and Robinson, *The Wonder of Being Human*, 36.

61. Eccles and Robinson, *The Wonder of Being Human*, 36.

62. Eccles and Robinson, *The Wonder of Being Human*, 38.

63. A.S. Eddington, *The Nature of the Physical World*, Gifford Lectures of 1927, annotated edition (Newcastle upon Tyne, UK: Cambridge Scholars Publishing, 2014): 336.

64. Willis Harman. "Commentary," *Brain/Mind Bulletin* 21:3 (1995): 4.

65. T. S. Ananthu, *Science Dynamics: A Newly Emerging Paradigm* (New Delhi: Gandhi Peace Foundation, 1987): 21.

66. Eccles and Robinson, *The Wonder of Being Human*, 53.

67. Etzel Cardeña, Steven J. Lynn, Stanley Krippner, eds., *Varieties of Anomalous Experience: Examining the Scientific Evidence* (Washington, DC: American Psychological Association, 2000).

68. Edward F. Kelly, et al, eds., *Irreducible Mind: Toward a Psychology for the 21st Century* (Lanham, MD: Rowman and Littlefield, 2007).

69. Dean Radin, *The Conscious Universe: The Scientific Truth of Psychic Phenomena* (San Francisco: Harper SanFrancisco, 1997).

70. Dean Radin *Entangled Minds: Extrasensory Experiences in a Quantum Reality.* (New York: Paraview/Simon & Schuster, 2006).

71. Robert Nadeau and Menas Kafatos, *The Non-local Universe: The New Physics and Matters of the* Mind (New York: Oxford UP, 1999): 65–82.

72. Herbert N. *Quantum Reality.* Garden City, NY: Anchor/Doubleday; 1987: 214.

73. Kafatos and Nadeau, *The Conscious Universe: Parts and Wholes in Physical Reality,* 127–129.

74. Huston Smith, Foreword, Ann Jauregui, *Epiphanies: Where Science and Miracles Meet* (New York: Atria, 2007): xiv.

75. Dean Radin, *Entangled Minds,* 208–239. See also Radin, *The Conscious Universe,* 289–297, and D. S. Kothari, "Atom and Self," The Meghnad Saha Medal Lecture, *Proceedings of the Indian National Science Academy,* Part A, Physical Science 46: 1 (1980): 1–28.

76. C. J. S. Clarke, "The Nonlocality of Mind," *Journal of Consciousness Studies* 2(3):327 (2003): 231–40. See also Larry Dossey, "Nonlocal Mind: A (Fairly) Brief History of the Term," *Explore* 11(2):89 (2015): 101.

77. Brian Olshansky and Larry Dossey, "Retroactive prayer: A Preposterous Hypothesis?" *British Medical Journal* 327 (December 20, 2003): 1465–68. See also William Braud, "Wellness Implications of Retroactive Intentional Influence: Exploring an Outrageous Hypothesis," *Alternative Therapies in Health & Medicine* 6:1 (2000): 37–48.

78. Julia Mossbridge, Patrizio Tressoldi, Jessica Utts, "Predictive physiological anticipation preceding seemingly unpredictable stimuli: a meta-analysis," *Frontiers in Psychology* 3 (2012):390. doi: 10.3389/fpsyg.2012.00390. http://www.frontiersin.org/Perception_Science/

10.3389/fpsyg.2012.00390/full. See also Larry Dossey, "Why Are Scientists Afraid of Daryl Bem?" *Explore (NY)* 7:3 (2011): 27–137; Charles Honorton and Diane C. Ferrari, "'Future telling': A meta-analysis of forced-choice precognition exeperiments, 1935–1987," *Journal of Parapsychology* 53 (1989):281–308; Patrizio E. Tressoldi, Massimiliano Martinelli, Luca Semenzato, "Pupil dilation prediction of random events," *F1000 Res.* 2 (2014): 262. http://dx.doi.org/10.12688/f1000research. 2-262.v2; and Patrizio E. Tressoldi, et al, "Let Your Eyes Predict: prediction accuracy of pupillary responses to random alerting and neutral sounds," *SAGE Open* 1:2 (2011): 1–7.

79. Stephen E. Braude, "Psi and the Nature of Abilities," *Journal of Parapsychology* 56:3 (September 1992): 205-228.

80. A. S. Eddington, *Science and the Unseen World.*

81. Olivier Costa deBeauregard, The Paranormal is Not Excluded from Physics," *Journal of Scientific Exploration*12:2 (1998):315–320.

82. Olivier Costa de Beauregard, "Wavelike Coherence and CPT Invariance: Sesames of the Paranormal," *Journal of Scientific Exploration* 16:4 (2002): 651–654.

83. George Wald, "Life and Mind in the Universe," *International Journal of Quantum Chemistry* 26:11 (April 16, 2008): 1–15.

84. George Wald, "Life and Mind in the Universe," *The Evolution of Consciousness*, ed. Kishore Gandhi, (New York: Free Press, 1983):19.

85. Henry P. Stapp, Harnessing Science and Religion: Implications of the New Scientific Conception of Human Beings," *Science & Theology News* 1:6 (February 2001): 8.

86. Gerald Feinberg, "Precognition—A Memory of Things Future," in *Quantum Physics and Parapsychology*, ed. Laura Oteri, (New York: Parapsychology Foundation, 1975): 54–73.

87. Henry Margenau quoted in Lawrence LeShan, *The Science of the Paranormal* (Northamptonshire, UK: Aquarian Press 1987): 118.

88. Vlatko Vedral, "Living in a Quantum World," *Scientific American* 304:6 (2011): 38–43.

89. Johann Summhammer. "Quantum cooperation of insects." ARXiv: quant-ph/0503136 vl. Last modified March 15, 2005. Accessed May 1, 2015.

http://arxiv.org/abs/quant-ph/0503136. Quoted in Dean Radin, *Entangled Minds,* 16–17.

90. Dean Radin, *Entangled Minds,* 235.

91. Patrizio E. Tressoldi, "Extraordinary Claims Require Extraordinary Evidence: The Case of Nonlocal Perception, a Classical and Bayesian Review of Evidences," *Frontiers of Quantitative Psychology and Measurement* 2 (2011): 117. doi10.3389/fpsyg,2011.00117. See also Stephan A. Schwartz, "Six Protocols, Neuroscience, and Near Death: An Emerging Paradigm Incorporating Nonlocal Consciousness," Academia.edu. Accessed 28 February, 2015. http://www.academia.edu/9540536/ Six_Protocols_Neuroscience_and_Near_Death_An_Emerging_ Paradigm_Incorporating_Nonlocal_Consciousness; Daryl J. Bem, et al., "Feeling the Future: A Meta-Analysis of 90 Experiments on the Anomalous Anticipation of Random Future Events," Social Science Research Network. Last modified August 4, 2015. Accessed March 11, 2015. http:// ssrn.com/abstract=2423692 or http://dx.doi.org/10.2139/ssrn.2423692; and Julia Mossbridge, Patrizio Tressoldi and Jessica Utts, "Predictive Physiological Anticipation Preceding Seemingly Unpredictable Stimuli: A Meta-Analysis," *Frontiers in Psychology* 3:390 (October 2012): 1–18, https://escholarship.org/uc/item/22b0b1js#page-1.

92. Edward F. Kelly, *Beyond Physicalism,* 542.

93. Matthew 23:24.

94. Voltaire, "La princesse de babylone," in *Romans et Contes* (Paris; Editions Garnier Frères, 1960): 366.

95. "Emily Dickinson," Brainyquote.com. Accessed 20 April, 2015. http:// www.brainyquote.com/quotes/quotes/e/emilydicki106414.html.

96. Lewis Thomas, *Lives of a Cell* (New York: Penguin, 1974): 141.

97. Alfred Lord Tennyson, "Flower in the Crannied Wall," Bartleby.com. Accessed March 31, 2015. http://www.bartleby.com/246/394.html.

98. George Eliot, *Middlemarch,* vol. 1, bk. 2, chap. 20. Schmoop.com. Accessed March 25, 2015. http://www.shmoop.com/march/ compassion-forgiveness-quotes.html.

99. Russell Targ and Harold E. Puthoff, *Mind-Reach: Scientists Look at Psychic Abilities* (New York: Delta, 1977): 169.

100. Edward F. Kelly and David E. Presti, *Beyond Physicalism*, 123.

101. David Darling, *Soul Search* (New York: Villard, 1997): 158.

102. Stephen King quoted in Naomi Epel, *Writers Dreaming* (New York: Carol Southern Books/Crown, 1993): 139.

103. Lawrence LeShan, *How to Meditate*. (Boston:: Little Brown, 1999).

104. Mary Oliver, "Sometimes" in *Red Bird: Poems* (Boston: Beacon Press, 2008): 35.

105. Gregory Bateson, *Steps to an Ecology of Mind* (San Francisco: Chandler Press, 1972); 467.

106. Ken Wilber, *Eye to Eye: The Quest for the New Paradigm* (Garden City, NY: Anchor/Doubleday, 1983): 234.

107. Lyall Watson, *Dreams of Dragons* (Rochester, VT: Destiny Books, 1992): 27.

108. Brian Inglis, *Natural and Supernatural: a History of the Paranormal From Earliest Times to 1914* (Dorset, UK: Prism Press, 1992): 158.

109. Lyall Watson, *Dreams of Dragons*, 27.

110. Walt Whitman, "Passage to India," st. 6, lines 110–115, *Leaves of Grass*. Bartleby.com. Accessed August 21, 2015. http://www.bartleby.com/142/183.html.

111. F. W. H. Myers quoted in Edward F. Kelly, et al., eds., *Beyond Physicalism*, xviii.

112. Erwin Schrödinger, *My View of the World*, Cecily Hastings, trans. (Woodbridge, CT: Ox Bow Press, 1983): 31–34

113. Erwin Schrödinger, *What is Life? And Mind and Matter* (London: Cambridge UP, 1969): 139, 145.

114. Erwin Schrödinger, *My View of the World*, 21–22.

115. A. S. Eddington, *The Nature of the Physical World*, 338.

116. Renée Weber, *Dialogues with Scientists and Sages* (New York: Routledge & Kegan Paul, 1986): 41.

117. David Bohm and Basil J. Hiley, *The Undivided Universe: An Ontological Interpretation of Quantum Theory* (London: Routledge, 1995): 389.

118. William Butler Yeats, "Ideas of Good and Evil" in *Irish Writing in the Twentieth Century,* ed. David Pierce (Cork, Ireland: Cork UP, 2000): 62.

119. Michael Grosso quoted in Edward F. Kelly, et al., eds. *Beyond Physicalism,* 83–84.

120. William James quoted in Edward F. Kelly, et al., eds. *Beyond Physicalism,* 521–522.

121. Paul Brunton quoted in Network Newsletter of the Scientific and Medical Network, UK 33 (April 1987): 18.

122. Aldous Huxley, *The Doors of Perception.* (London: Chatto and Windus; 1954. Reprint: London, UK: Granada Publishing; 1984: 19–20.

123. David Darling, *Soul Search,* 154–166.

124. Michael Grosso quoted in Edward F. Kelly, et al., eds. *Beyond Physicalism,* 84–85.

125. Michael Grosso, *Soulmaking* (Charlottesville, VA: Hampton Roads, 1997): 85.

126. "Srinivasa Ramanujan." Wikipedia. Accessed April 20, 2015. http://en.wikipedia.org/wiki/Srinivasa_Ramanujan.

127. F. W. H. Myers quoted in Edward F. Kelly, et al., eds. *Beyond Physicalism,* 26.

128. Joseph Chilton Pearce, *Evolution's End* (San Francisco: HarperSanFrancisco, 1992): 8–9.

129. Neil Baldwin, *Edison: Inventing the Century* (New York: Hyperion, 1995): 376.

130. Eugene Wigner quoted in *Toward a Unity of Knowledge: Psychological Issues* 6:2:22, ed. Marjorie Greene (New York: International UP, 1969): 45.

131. Carl Friedrich von Weizsäcker, Introduction, Gopi Krishna, *The Biological Basis of Religion and Genius* (New York: Harper and Row, 1972): 35–36.

132. F. X. Charet, *Spiritualism and the Foundations of C. G. Jung's Psychology* (Albany, NY: SUNY Press, 1993): 61.

133. Aldous Huxley, *Tomorrow and Tomorrow and Tomorrow* (New York: Signet, 1964): 32.

134. Huston Smith, *Forgotten Truth,* 113.

135. Vivekananda and Bastami quoted in Huston Smith, *Forgotten Truth,* 113–114.

136. Hal Hellman, *Great Feuds in Science* (New York: John Wiley, 1998).

137. Edward C. Bullard. "The Emergence of Plate Tectonics: A Personal View," *Annual Review of Earth and Planetary Sciences* 3 (1975): 5.

138. Max Planck, *Scientific Autobiography,* Frank Gaynor, trans., (London: Williams & Norgate, 1950): 33–34.

139. Antonio Damasio quoted in Edward E. Kelly, et al, eds., *Irreducible Mind,* xx.

140. Stan V. McDaniel, Book review of Matthew Colborn, *Pluralism and the Mind: Consciousness, Worldviews, and the Limits of Science, Journal of Scientific Exploration* 26:3 (2012): 657–661.

141. Rupert Sheldrake, *A New Science of Life: The Hypothesis of Formative Causation* (Los Angeles: Jeremy Tarcher, 1981); see also Tim Adams, "Rupert Sheldrake: the "heretic" at odds with scientific dogma," *The Guardian,* February 4, 2012. Accessed March 2, 2015. http://www.theguardian.com/science/2012/feb/05/rupert-sheldrake-interview-science-delusion.

142. Walter Moore, *A Life of Erwin Schrödinger* (Cambridge, UK: Cambridge UP, 1994): 181.

143. J.W.N. Sullivan, "Interviews with the Great Scientists VI: Max Planck," *The Observer* (London), Jan. 25, 1931, 17.

144. "Max Planck." Wikiquote. Accessed April 15, 2015. http://en.wikiquote.org/wiki/Max_Planck.

145. Carl G. Jung, *Psychology and Religion: West and East,* vol. 11 of *The Collected Works of C. G. Jung,* eds. Sir Herbert Read and Gerhard Adler, R. F. C. Hull, trans (Princeton, NJ: Princeton UP, 1975): 12.

146. Lewis Thomas, *Lives of a Cell* (New York: Penguin, 1978): 52.

147. Lewis Thomas, *Lives of a Cell,* 142.

148. Arthur Koestler, *Janus: A Summing Up* (New York: Random House, 1978): 282.

Consciousness is Mind Beyond Space and Time: The New Paradigm

1. Ervin Laszlo, *Quantum Shift in the Global Brain: How the New Scientific Reality Can Change Us and Our World* (Rochester, VT: Inner Traditions, 2008), 163.

2. Russell Targ, Harold E. Puthoff, *Mind-Reach: Scientists Look at Psychic Abilities* (New York: Delacorte, 1977).

3. Kenneth Ring and Sharon Cooper, "Near-Death and Out-of-Body Experiences in the Blind: A Study of Apparent Eyeless Vision," *Journal of Near-Death Studies* 16:12 (Winter 1997): 101–147.

4. Ring and Cooper, 140.

5. This case and others like it are reviewed in Ervin Laszlo with Anthony Peake, *The Immortal Mind* (Rochester, VT: Inner Traditions, 2014).

6. Michael B. Sabom, *Light and Death: One Doctor's Fascinating Account of Near-Death Experiences* (Grand Rapids, MI: Zondervan Publishing, 1998).

7. Laszlo with Peake.

8. Rosemary Brown, *Immortals at My Elbow* (London: Bachman & Turner, 1974).

9. Bill Guggenheim, Judy Guggenheim, *Hello from Heaven: A New Field of Research-After-Death Communication Confirms That Life and Love Are Eternal* (New York: Bantam, 1996).

10. Stanislav Grof, *Modern Consciousness Research and the Understanding of Art* (Santa Cruz, CA: Multidisciplinary Association for Psychedelic Studies, 2015).

11. Roger Sperry, quoted in Denis Brian, *Genius Talk: Conversations with Nobel Scientists and Other Luminaries* (Amsterdam: Kluwer Academic Publishers, 1995): 367.

12. Eugene P. Wigner, "Are We Machines?" in *Proceedings of the American Philosophical Society* 113:2 (April 1969): 95–101.

13. Various theories attempt to explain how information could be conveyed to the brain at the quantum level, including the much-discussed Orchestrated Objective Reduction theory of Roger Penrose and Stuart

Hameroff. See Penrose, et al, *Consciousness and the Universe: Quantum Physics, Evolution, Brain & Mind* (Cosmology Science Publishers, 2011).

14. William James, *Ingersoll Lecture on Immortality* (Boston: Houghton Mifflin, 1899).

15. David Bohm, *Wholeness and the Implicate Order* (London: Routledge & Kegan Paul, 1980); Jacob Bekenstein, "Information in the Holographic Universe" in *Scientific American* 289 (2003): 58–65.

16. Masanori Hanada, et al., "Holographic Description of a Quantum Black Hole on a Computer" in *Science* 344:6186 (April 2014): 882–885.

17. Edgar Mitchell, "Nature's Mind: The Quantum Hologram" in *International Journal of Computing Anticipatory Systems* 7 (2000): 295–312.

18. The holofield theory is discussed in greater detail in Ervin Laszlo with Alexander Laszlo, *Consciousness Beyond Space and Time* (New York: Select Books, 2016, unpublished).

19. Ervin Laszlo with Gyorgyi Szabo, "The Oneness Declaration: Sixteen Hallmarks of the New Consciousness," *Humanity's Team*. Accessed August 17, 2015. http://www.humanitysteam.org/ErvinLaszlo.

Bibliography of Authors' Works

STANLEY KRIPPNER

Advances in Parapsychological Research, Vols.1-9. Volumes 1-9 published in various editions between 1977 and 2014. Volumes 1-3 originally published in New York by Plenum Press. Volumes 4-9 originally published in Jefferson, NC, by McFarland & Company.

Varieties of Anomalous Experience: Examining the Scientific Evidence, Second Edition, with Etzel Cardeña and Steven J. Lynn. Washington, DC: American Psychological Association, 2014.

Post-Traumatic Stress Disorder, with Daniel B. Pitchford and Jeannine Davies. Santa Barbara, CA: Greenwood, 2012.

The Voice of Rolling Thunder: A Medicine Man's Wisdom for Walking the Red Road, with Sidian Morning Star Jones. Rochester, VT: Bear & Co., 2012.

Demystifying Shamans and Their World: A Multidisciplinary Study, with Adam J. Rock. Luton: Andrews UK, 2011.

Debating Psychic Experience: Human Potential or Human Illusion? with Harris L. Friedman. Santa Barbara, CA: ABC-CLIO, 2010.

Haunted by Combat: Understanding PTSD in War Veterans, with Daryl S. Paulson. Lanham: Rowman & Littlefield Publishers, 2010.

Mysterious Minds: The Neurobiology of Psychics, Mediums, and Other Extraordinary People, with Harris L. Friedman. Santa Barbara, CA: Praeger, 2010.

Perchance to Dream: The Frontiers of Dream Psychology, with Debbie Joffe-Ellis. New York: Nova Science Publishers, 2009.

Personal Mythology: Using Ritual, Dreams, and Imagination to Discover Your Inner Story, with David Feinstein. Santa Rosa, CA: Energy Psychology Press/Elite Books, 2008.

Healing Stories: The Use of Narrative in Counseling and Psychotherapy, with Michael Bova and Leslie Gray. Charlottesville, VA: Puente Publications, 2007.

Healing Tales: The Narrative Arts in Spiritual Traditions. Charlottesville, CA: Puente Publications, 2007.

Becoming Psychic: Spiritual Lessons for Focusing Your Hidden Abilities, with Stephen Kierulff.

Franklin Lakes, NJ: New Page Books, 2004.

The Psychological Impact of War Trauma on Civilians: An International Perspective, with Teresa M. McIntyre. Westport, CT: Praeger, 2003.

Extraordinary Dreams and How to Work with Them, with Fariba Bogzaran and André Pércia de Carvalho. Albany: SUNY Press, 2002.

Dream Telepathy: Experiments in Nocturnal Extrasensory Perception, with Montague Ullman and Alan Vaughan. Charlottesville, VA: Hampton Roads, 2001.

Dreamscaping: New and Creative Ways to Work with Your Dreams, with Mark Robert Waldman. Los Angeles: Roxbury Park/Lowell House, 1999.

Broken Images, Broken Selves: Dissociative Narratives in Clinical Practice, with Susan Marie Powers. Washington, DC: Brunner/Mazel, 1997.

Spiritual Dimensions of Healing, with Patrick Welch. New York: Irvington Publishers, 1992.

Dreamtime and Dreamwork: Decoding the Language of the Night. New York: St. Martin's Press, 1990.

Dreamworking: How to Use Your Dreams for Creative Problem Solving, with Joseph Dillard. Buffalo, NY: Bearly, 1988.

Personal Mythology: The Psychology of Your Evolving Self, with David Feinstein. New York: St. Martin's Press, 1988.

Healing States: A Journey into the World of Spiritual Healing and Shamanism, with Alberto Villoldo. New York: Simon & Schuster, 1987.

Human Possibilities: Mind Exploration in the USSR and Eastern Europe. Garden City, NY: Anchor Press/Doubleday, 1980.

Psychoenergetic Systems: The Interaction of Consciousness, Energy, and Matter, with Mary Calley Carlson. New York: Gordon and Breach, 1979.

The Realms of Healing, with Alberto Villoldo. Millbrae, CA: Celestial Arts, 1976.

Song of the Siren: A Parapsychological Odyssey. New York: Harper & Row, 1975.

The Energies of Consciousness: Explorations in Acupuncture, Auras, and Kirlian Photography, with Daniel Rubin. New York: Gordon and Breach, 1975.

The Kirlian Aura: Photographing the Galaxies of Life, with Daniel Rubin. Garden City, NY: Anchor Books, 1974.

JEAN HOUSTON

The Wizard of Us: Transformational Lessons from Oz. New York: Atria Books, 2012.

The Hero and the Goddess: The Odyssey as Pathway to Personal Transformation. Wheaton, IL: Quest Books, 2009.

The Power of Yin: Celebrating Female Consciousness, with Hazel Henderson and Barbara Marx Hubbard. New York: Cosimo Books, reissue edition, 2007.

Jump Time: Shaping Your Future in a World of Radical Change. Boulder, CO: Sentient Publications, 2004.

Mystical Dogs: Animals as Guides to Our Inner Life. Makawao, HI: Inner Ocean, 2002.

Mind Games: The Guide to Inner Space (second edition), with Robert Masters, Wheaton, IL: Quest Books, 1995.

The Passion of Isis and Osiris: A Gateway to Transcendent Love. New York: Ballantine Books, 1998.

A Passion for the Possible: A Guide to Realizing Your True Potential. San Francisco: HarperSanFrancisco, 1997.

The Possible Human: A Course in Enhancing Your Physical, Mental, and Creative Abilities. New York: J. P. Tarcher/Putnam, 1997.

The Search for the Beloved: Journeys in Mythology and Sacred Psychology. New York: J. P. Tarcher/Putnam, 1997.

A Mythic Life: Learning to Live Our Greater Story, with a Foreword by Mary Catherine Bateson. San Francisco: HarperSanFrancisco, 1996.

Manual for the Peacemaker: An Iroquois Legend to Heal Self and Society, with Margaret Rubin. Wheaton, IL: Quest Books, 1995.

Public Like a Frog: Entering the Lives of Three Great Americans. Wheaton, IL: Quest Books, 1993.

A Feminine Myth of Creation, with Diana Vandenberg, Den Hague: J. H. Gottmer, 1992.

Godseed: The Journey of Christ. Wheaton, IL: Quest Books, 1992.

The Hero and the Goddess: The Odyssey as Mystery and Initiation. New York: Ballantine Books, 1992.

Life-force: The Psycho-Historical Recovery of the Self. New York: Delacorte Press, 1980.

Listening to the Body, with Robert Masters. New York: Dell Publishing, 1978.

Executive Mansions and Capitols of America, with Price Daniel. Wakusha, WI: Putnam, 1969.

Psychedelic Art, with Robert Master. New York: Grove, 1967.

The Varieties of Psychedelic Experience, with Robert Masters, New York: Holt, Rinehart and Winston, 1966.

LARRY DOSSEY

One Mind: How Our Individual Mind Is Part of a Greater Consciousness and Why It Matters. Carlsbad, CA: Hay House, 2013.

The Science of Premonitions: How to Know the Future Can Help Us Avoid Danger, Maximize Opportunities, and Create a Better Life. New York: Plume, 2009.

The Extraordinary Healing Power of Ordinary Things: Fourteen Natural Steps to Health and Happiness. New York: Harmony Books, 2006.

The Power of Premonitions: How Knowing the Future Can Shape Our Lives. Brilliance Publishing, 2005.

Healing Beyond the Body: Medicine and the Infinite Reach of the Mind. Boston: Shambhala, 2001.

Reinventing Medicine: Beyond Mind-Body to a New Era of Healing. San Francisco: HarperSanFrancisco, 1999.

Be Careful What You Pray For—You Just Might Get It: What We Can Do about the Unintentional Effects of Our Thoughts, Prayers, and Wishes. San Francisco: HarperSanFrancisco, 1997.

Prayer Is Good Medicine: How to Reap the Healing Benefits of Prayer. San Francisco: HarperSanFrancisco, 1996.

Larry Dossey in Conversation with Michael Toms. Lower Lake, CA: Asian Pub, 1994.

Meaning and Medicine: Lessons from a Doctor's Tales of Breakthrough and Healing. New York: Bantam Books, 1991.

Recovering the Soul: A Scientific and Spiritual Search. New York: Bantam Books, 1989.

Beyond Illness: Discovering the Experience of Health. New York: Random House, 1984.

Space, Time, and Medicine. New York: Random House, 1982.

Ervin Laszlo

The Immortal Mind: Science and the Continuity of Consciousness beyond the Brain, with Anthony Peake. Rochester, VT: Inner Traditions, 2014.

The Self-Actualizing Cosmos: The Akasha Revolution in Science and Human Consciousness. Rochester, VT: Inner Traditions, 2014.

Dawn of the Akashic Age: New Consciousness, Quantum Resonance, and the Future of the World. Rochester, VT: Inner Traditions, 2013.

The Akasha Paradigm: Revolution in Science, Evolution in Consciousness. Waterside Publications, 2012.

Simply Genius! And Other Tales from My Life. Carlsbad, CA: Hay House, 2011.

Chaos Point 2012 and Beyond: Our Choices Between Global Disaster and a Sustainable Planet. Charlottesville, VA: Hamptons Road Publishing Company, 2010.

The Akashic Experience: Science and the Cosmic Memory Field. Rochester, VT: Inner Traditions, 2009.

WorldShift 2012: Making Green Business, New Politics, and Higher Conscious-ness Work Together. Rochester, VT: Inner Traditions, 2009.

CosMos: A Co-Creator's Guide to the Whole World. Carlsbad, CA: Hay House, 2008.

Quantum Shift in the Global Brain: How the New Scientific Reality Can Change Us and Our World. Rochester, VT: Inner Traditions, 2008.

Global Survival: The Challenge and Its Implications for Thinking and Acting, with Peter Seidel. New York: SelectBooks, 2006.

Science and the Reenchantment of the Cosmos: The Rise of the Integral Vision of Reality. Rochester, VT: Inner Traditions, 2006.

The Chaos Point: The World at the Crossroads. Hampton Roads, 2006.

Science and the Akashic Field: An Integral Theory of Everything. Rochester, VT: Inner Traditions, 2004.

The Connectivity Hypothesis: Foundations of an Integral Science of Quantum, Cosmos, Life, and Consciousness. Albany: State University of New York Press, 2003.

The Consciousness Revolution, with Stanislav Grof and Peter Russell. Las Vegas: Elf Rock Publications, 2003.

You Can Change the World: The Global Citizen's Handbook for Living on Planet Earth. New York: Select Books, 2003.

You Can Change the World: An Action Handbook for the 21st Century. Clun: Positive News, 2002.

Macroshift: Navigating the Transformation to a Sustainable World. San Fran-cisco: Berrett-Koehler, 2001.

The Consciousness Revolution: A Transatlantic Dialogue, with Stanislav Grof, Ervin Laszlo, and Peter Russell. Boston: Element, 1999.

The Insight Edge: An Introduction to the Theory and Practice of Evolutionary Management. Westport, CT: Quorum, 1997.

Third Millennium: The Challenge and the Vision. Stroud: Gaia Books, 1997.

Changing Visions: Human Cognitive Maps: Past, Present, and Future. West-port, CT: Praeger, 1996.

Evolution: The General Theory. Cresskill, NJ: Hampton Press, 1996.

The Systems View of the World: A Holistic Vision for Our Time. Cresskill, NJ: Hampton Press, 1996.

The Whispering Pond: A Personal Guide to the Emerging Vision of Science. Rockport, MA: Element Books, Ltd., 1996.

The Interconnected Universe: Conceptual Foundations of Transdisciplinary Unified Theory. River Edge, NJ: World Scientific, 1995.

The Choice: Evolution or Extinction? A Thinking Person's Guide to Global Issues. New York: J. P. Tarcher/Putnam, 1994.

Vision 2020: Reordering Chaos for Global Survival. Langhorne, PA: Gordon and Breach, 1994.

The Creative Cosmos: A Unified Science of Matter, Life, and Mind. Edinburgh: Floris Books, 1993.

The Evolution of Cognitive Maps: New Paradigms for the Twenty-First Century. Langhorne, PA: Gordon and Breach, 1993.

The Age of Bifurcation: Understanding the Changing World. Philadelphia: Gordon and Breach, 1991.

The New Evolutionary Paradigm. New York: Gordon and Breach, 1991.

Inner Limits of Mankind: Heretical Reflections on Today's Values, Culture, and Politics. London: Oneworld, 1989.

Evolution: The Grand Synthesis. Boston: New Science Library, 1987.

Systems Science and World Order: Selected Studies. New York: Pergamon Press, 1983.

Political and Institutional Issues of the New International Economic Order. New York: Pergamon Press, 1981.

Regional Cooperation among Developing Countries: The New Imperative of Development in the 1980s. New York: Pergamon Press, 1981.

The Obstacles to the New International Economic Order. New York: Pergamon Press, 1980.

The Structure of the World Economy and Prospects for a New International Economic Order, with Joel Kurtzman. New York: Pergamon Press, 1980.

The United States, Canada, and the New International Economic Order, with Joel Kurtzman. New York: Pergamon Press, 1979.

The Objectives of the New International Economic Order. New York: Pergamon Press, 1978.

Goals for Mankind: A Report to the Club of Rome on the New Horizons of Global Community. New York: Dutton, 1977.

A Strategy for the Future: The Systems Approach to World Order. New York: George Braziller, 1974.

The World System: Models, Norms, Applications. New York: G. Braziller, 1973.

Value Theory in Philosophy and Social Science. New York: Gordon and Breach, 1973.

Introduction to Systems of Philosophy: Toward a New Paradigm of Contemporary Thought. New York: Gordon and Breach, 1972.

The Systems View of the World: The Natural Philosophy of the New Developments in the Sciences. New York: George Braziller, 1972.

Human Values and Natural Science. New York: Gordon and Breach, 1970.

System, Structure, and Experience: Toward a Scientific Theory of Mind. New York: Gordon and Breach, 1969.

Philosophy in the Soviet Union: A Survey of the Mid-Sixties. New York: Praeger, 1967.

Beyond Skepticism and Realism. A Constructive Exploration of Husserlian and Whiteheadian Methods of Inquiry. The Hague: Martinus Nijhoff, 1966.

Individualism, Collectivism, and Political Power: A Relational Analysis of Ideological Conflict. The Hague: Martinus Nijhoff, 1963.

Essential Society: An Ontological Reconstruction. The Hague: Martinus Nijhoff, 1963.

Index

About the Authors

ERVIN LASZLO

Ervin Laszlo spent his childhood in Budapest. He was a celebrated child prodigy, with public appearances from the age of nine. Upon receiving a Grand Prize at the international music competition in Geneva, he was allowed to cross the Iron Curtain and begin an international concert career, first in Europe and then in the United States. At the request of Senator Claude Pepper of Florida, he was awarded United States citizenship by an Act of Congress before his twenty-first birthday.

Laszlo received the Sorbonne's highest degree, the Doctorat ès Lettres et Sciences Humaines, in 1970. Shifting to the life of a scientist and humanist, he lectured at various American universities, including Yale, Princeton, Northwestern, the University of Houston, and the State University of New York. The author, co-author or editor of ninety-one books, which have appeared in twenty-four languages, Laszlo has also written several hundred papers and articles in scientific journals and popular magazines. He is a member of numerous scientific bodies, including the International Academy of Science, the World Academy of Arts and Science, the International Academy of Philosophy of Science, and the International Medici Academy. Laszlo received the Goi Peace Award in 2001, the Assisi Mandir of Peace Prize in 2006, the Polyhistor Prize of Hungary in 2015 and was nominated for the Nobel Peace Prize in 2004 and 2005. He was elected member of the Hungarian Academy of Science in 2010.

Laszlo is founder and president of the global think tank The Club of Budapest and Founder and Director of the Laszlo Institute of New Paradigm Research in Italy.

JEAN HOUSTON

Jean Houston, PhD, scholar, philosopher, and researcher in Human Capacities, is the author of twenty-six books, including *Jump Time, A Passion for the Possible, Search for the Beloved, Life Force, The Possible Human, Public Like a Frog, A Mythic Life: Learning to Live Our Greater Story,* and *Manual of the Peacemaker.*

As advisor to UNICEF in human and cultural development, Dr. Houston has worked around the world helping to implement extensive educational programs. In September 1999, she traveled to Dharamsala, India with a group chosen to work with the Dalai Lama in a learning and advisory capacity. Dr. Houston has also served in an advisory capacity to President Bill Clinton and Hillary Clinton, as well as assisting Mrs. Clinton in writing her book *It Takes a Village: And Other Lessons Children Teach Us.* Since 2003, Dr. Houston has been working with the United Nations Development Program, training leaders in human and cultural development.

Together with other international agencies and companies, over the last forty-five years, she has worked in more than one hundred countries. In 2008, the Jean Houston Foundation was formed to teach Social Artistry, a community-leadership training program that she developed, in the United States and overseas. This training has been conducted in Albania, the eastern Caribbean, Kenya, Zambia, Nepal, and the Philippines. Dr. Houston has worked intensively in forty cultures helping to enhance and deepen their own uniqueness while they become part of the global community.

LARRY DOSSEY

Larry Dossey, MD, is an internist and author of twelve books on the relationships between consciousness, spirituality, and healing, including *Space, Time & Medicine; Reinventing Medicine*; the *New York Times* best seller *Healing Words: The Power of Prayer and the Practice of Medicine; The Power of Premonitions*; and *One Mind: How Our Individual Mind Is Part of a Greater Consciousness and Why It Matters*. His books have been translated into languages around the world.

Dr. Dossey is the former chief of staff of Medical City Dallas Hospital; former co-chair of the Panel on Mind/Body Interventions, National Center for Complementary and Alternative Medicine, National Institutes of Health; and executive editor of *Explore: The Journal of Science and Healing*. He lives in northern New Mexico with his wife, Barbara, an award-winning author and nurse-educator. He lectures around the world.

STANLEY KRIPPNER

Stanley Krippner, PhD, is professor of psychology at Saybrook University, Fellow in four APA divisions, and past president of two divisions (30 and 32). He is co-author of *Extraordinary Dreams, The Mythic Path*, and *Haunted by Combat: Understanding PTSD in War Veterans*. Dr. Krippner has conducted workshops and seminars on dreams and hypnosis in Argentina,

Brazil, Canada, China, Colombia, Cuba, Cyprus, Ecuador, Finland, France, Germany, Great Britain, Italy, Japan, Lithuania, Mexico, the Netherlands, Panama, the Philippines, Portugal, Puerto Rico, Russia, South Africa, Spain, Sweden, and Venezuela, and at the last four congresses of the InterAmerican Psychological Association.